"This book is a must-have for practitioners currently implementing an RTI or MTSS framework in their schools. The authors have aptly translated the existing evidence base to provide numerous practical strategies and resources that will immediately increase rigor in the classroom."

Matt Hoskins, Data Analyst and State Implementation
Specialist, Exceptional Children Division,
North Carolina Department of Public Instruction

"*Rigor in the RTI and MTSS Classroom* is groundbreaking in several facets! Finally, one place for educators to find practical information and strategies to use the next day around rigor, collaboration, data-based decision making, instructional strategies, and many more critical components of effective MTSS and RTI frameworks! The authors pull from REAL people doing REAL work within these frameworks every day, not just theory or past research. It puts educational leaders on notice that they are one of the most critical and greatest predictors of their school's success! The reflection questions are also a great included tool, whether for an individual reader or a book study group. Great work, Dr. Blackburn and Dr. Witzel!!"

Todd Wiedemann, MSEd, Assistant Director,
Kansas MTSS

Rigor in the RTI and MTSS Classroom

In this new book, best-selling author Barbara R. Blackburn and intervention expert Bradley S. Witzel show you how to develop rigorous RTI and MTSS programs that will support students and lead them to lasting success. Written in a clear, engaging style, *Rigor in the RTI and MTSS Classroom* offers an in-depth discussion of the issues facing students with academic problems as well as practical strategies for all teachers. You'll discover how to:

- Improve academic and social-emotional performance with scaffolding and demonstration of learning techniques;
- Establish and teach class rules, expectations, and consequences;
- Use evidence-based activities to spark student discussion;
- Implement rigorous, research-based strategies for math, literacy, reading, and writing development;
- Assess student growth and encourage self-reflection;
- Form an MTSS leadership team to ensure that student needs are met across building and district levels.

Each chapter contains anecdotes from schools across the country as well as a variety of ready-to-use tools and activities. Many of the tools are offered as free eResources at www.routledge.com/9781138193383, so you can easily print and distribute them for classroom use.

Dr. Barbara R. Blackburn, one of Global Gurus' top 30 educational professionals for 2016 and 2017, is the best-selling author of 17 books and an international speaker and consultant. She was an award-winning professor at Winthrop University and has taught students of all ages.

Dr. Bradley S. Witzel is a professor and director of the online M.Ed. in Intervention program in the College of Education at Winthrop University. He has worked as a classroom teacher and, before that, as a paraeducator in multiple secondary settings. A best-selling author and a respected speaker, he has over 50 publications, including 10 books, and has delivered nearly 500 conference and workshop presentations focusing on nontraditional learners.

This book is co-published with the Council for Exceptional Children (CEC), a professional association of educators dedicated to advancing the success of children with exceptionalities. CEC accomplishes its mission through advocacy, standards, and professional development. CEC represents all disciplines in the field, including teachers, early interventionists, administrators, researchers, and higher education faculty who are preparing the next generation of special educators.

Also Available From Eye on Education

(www.routledge.com/eyeoneducation)

Rigor for Students with Special Needs
Barbara R. Blackburn and Bradley Witzel

Rigor and Assessment in the Classroom
Barbara R. Blackburn

Motivating Struggling Learners:
10 Ways to Build Student Success
Barbara R. Blackburn

Rigor and Differentiation in the Classroom
Barbara R. Blackburn

Rigor in Your Classroom:
A Toolkit for Teachers
Barbara R. Blackburn

Rigor Is Not a Four-Letter Word, Third Edition
Barbara R. Blackburn

Rigor Made Easy:
Getting Started
Barbara R. Blackburn

Rigor in Your School: A Toolkit for Teachers
Ronald Williamson and Barbara R. Blackburn

Classroom Instruction from A to Z, Second Edition:
How to Promote Student Learning
Barbara R. Blackburn

The Principalship from A to Z, Second Edition
Barbara R. Blackburn with Ronald Williamson

Advocacy from A to Z
Robert Blackburn, Barbara R. Blackburn, and Ronald Williamson

Literacy from A to Z
Barbara R. Blackburn

Rigor in the RTI and MTSS Classroom

Practical Tools and Strategies

Barbara R. Blackburn
and Bradley S. Witzel

Council for
Exceptional
Children
The voice and vision of special education

Routledge
Taylor & Francis Group

NEW YORK AND LONDON

First published 2018
by Routledge
711 Third Avenue, New York, NY 10017

and by Routledge
2 Park Square, Milton Park, Abingdon, Oxon, OX14 4RN

Routledge is an imprint of the Taylor & Francis Group, an informa business

© 2018 Taylor & Francis

Library of Congress Cataloging-in-Publication Data
A catalog record for this book has been requested

ISBN: 978-1-138-19337-6 (hbk)
ISBN: 978-1-138-19338-3 (pbk)
ISBN: 978-1-315-63940-6 (ebk)

Typeset in Palatino and Formata
by Apex Covantage, LLC

Visit the eResources: www.routledge.com/9781138193383

Dedication

From Barbara:
To my brother-in-law, John, who is an encouragement to all those around him.

From Brad:
To my wife and children, who support my work around the country.

Council for Exceptional Children

About the Council for Exceptional Children

The Council for Exceptional Children (CEC) is a professional association of educators dedicated to advancing the success of children with exceptionalities. CEC accomplishes its mission through advocacy, standards, and professional development. CEC represents all disciplines in the field, including teachers, early interventionists, administrators, researchers, and higher education faculty who are preparing the next generation of special educators.

Advocacy

CEC works to ensure that the needs of special educators and early interventionists, and the children and youth they serve, are heard and heeded by policy makers, and engages an active grassroots advocacy network to advance CEC's critical policy messages.

Professional Standards

CEC advances standards that provide benchmarks for developing or revising policy and procedures for program accreditation, entry-level licensure, professional practice, and continuing professional growth.

Professional Resources

CEC supports the vision of well-prepared special educators teaching all children and youth. CEC works to enhance the knowledge, skills, diversity and cultural competency of the profession by providing the resources its members need, including:

- ◆ An annual Convention & Expo that is the premier gathering of special and gifted educators and early interventionists in the world.
- ◆ *Exceptional Children*, the premier research journal in the field of special education.
- ◆ *TEACHING Exceptional Children*, a leading trade publication that translates research into effective classroom practice.

Units and Special Interest Divisions

CEC members network, learn, and share within state and provincial units in the United States and Canada. CEC's 18 special interest divisions focus on the most critical issues in special education: developmental disabilities and autism; behavioral disorders; administration; diagnostic services; communicative disabilities and deafness; cultural and linguistic diversity; early childhood; learning disabilities; physical, health and multiple disabilities; research; global issues; visual and performing arts; career development and transition; visual impairments; gifted education; teacher education; and technology.

Council for Exceptional Children
2900 Crystal Drive, Suite 100
Arlington, VA 22202
888-232-7733
www.cec.sped.org

Acknowledgments

To Lauren Davis, our editor: You have a gift for knowing how to take our ideas and help us communicate them effectively.

To Jennifer Gennerman, Ted Gennerman, Matt Hoskins, Grace Pannell, David Putnam, Dean Richards, and Todd Wiedemann: Thank you for your amazing amount of input and suggestions, which helped us clarify and refine the content. This wouldn't have happened without you.

To Emma Capel: thank you for a wonderful cover design.

To Apex: thanks for the great job you did in page makeup.

To the teachers and leaders in our workshops and all those who read our books and use the ideas to impact students, thank you. You make a difference every day in the lives of your students.

From Barbara:

To my husband, Pete. You are the love of my life and you inspire me daily.

Thank you to my family—Dad, Mom, Becky, Brenda, and Hunter—for your continuing support.

From Brad:

Thank you to my Intervention students/teachers who continue to push for answers and challenge what we "know" from research. Never stop fighting to give your students the best education that they can receive. Children deserve the best, and you consistently make sure they get it.

Contents

eResources

As you read this book, you'll notice the eResources icon 🔻 next to the following tools. The icon indicates that these tools are available as free downloads on our website, www.routledge.com/9781138193383, so you can easily print and distribute them to your students.

Meet the Authors

Barbara R. Blackburn, Ph.D., has dedicated her life to raising the level of rigor and motivation for professional educators and students alike. What differentiates Barbara's 17 books are her easily executable concrete examples based on decades of experience as a teacher, professor, and consultant. Barbara's dedication to education was inspired in her early years by her parents, Bob and Rose. Her father's doctorate and lifetime career as a professor taught her the importance of professional training. Her mother's career as a school secretary shaped Barbara's appreciation of the effort all staff play in the education of every child.

Barbara has taught early childhood, elementary, middle, and high school students and has served as an educational consultant for three publishing companies. She holds a master's degree in school administration and was certified as a teacher and a school principal in North Carolina. She received her doctorate in Curriculum and Teaching from the University of North Carolina at Greensboro. In 2006, she received the award for Outstanding Junior Professor at Winthrop University. She left her position at the University of North Carolina at Charlotte to write and speak full-time.

A keynote presenter for the Australia Council for School Leaders, Barbara was recently named one of Global Gurus' Top 30 Education Gurus and speaks at state and national conferences, as well as regularly presenting workshops for teachers and administrators in elementary, middle, and high schools. Her workshops are lively, engaging, filled with practical information, and based on her 17 books. Her most popular topics include:

- Rigor Is Not a Four-Letter Word.
- Rigor for Students With Special Needs.
- Rigor and Assessment in the Classroom.
- Increasing Rigor Through Assessment of Student Work.
- Rigorous Schools and Classrooms: Leading the Way.
- Motivating Struggling Learners: 10 Strategies for Student Success.
- Instructional Strategies That Motivate Students.
- Train-the-Trainer Models of All Sessions.

For more information, or to schedule professional development, please contact her at her website: www.barbarablackburnonline.com

Bradley S. Witzel, Ph.D., is an award-winning teacher and researcher who works as a professor and director of the M.Ed. in Intervention program at Winthrop University, the flagship education college for the state of South Carolina. As a classroom teacher, he worked in multiple settings, teaching mainly math and science to high-achieving students with disabilities and at-risk concerns. Brad has authored more than 50 publications, including the recently published book *Teaching Elementary Mathematics to Struggling Learners* (Guilford Press), and edited the book *Bridging the Gap Between Arithmetic and Algebra* (Council for Exceptional Children). A popular professional developer, he has delivered nearly 500 workshop, conference, and video presentations on intervention delivery and mathematics. He has served as a member of multiple state-level MTSS and RTI governing boards and works with districts on guidance documents to guide educators through MTSS processes. Most importantly, he is a father of two, husband of an educator, and son of two educators.

Introduction

You might be wondering why Brad and Barbara wrote a book combining rigor and RTI/MTSS. This book has been in the planning stages for a few years. Brad's expertise is in working with students with learning disabilities and at-risk concerns, and he has collaborated with numerous states and districts on their RTI and MTSS programs. In doing so, one question continues to arise: How do we make sure, especially in today's accountability climate, that our students are working at rigorous levels?

Barbara has been researching, writing, and providing professional development on rigor since 2001. As she has worked with teachers, the same question was posed: How do we ensure rigor for all our students, including those with special needs? So, Brad and Barbara decided to collaborate and integrate those two issues in a way that would give teachers and leaders practical strategies to ensure success for all students.

This book was written for several potential audiences. First, there are educators who are intimately involved in the RTI/MTSS programs in their schools. If you fall into that group, we hope you will find information that will enhance your efforts. Next, there are core teachers who are struggling with how to ensure that students who need extra support receive it in their classrooms, with the hope that they can prevent students from needing to move into tiers 2 and 3. For you, we have provided key information about RTI/MTSS, along with instructional and assessment strategies that will inform core instruction at rigorous levels. Finally, some readers are leaders who want information on how they are meeting specialized needs of RTI/MTSS students without sacrificing rigor they can share with teachers and other stakeholders. Throughout the book, you will find that information, written in a practical way that can be easily communicated.

Why Should I Keep Reading?

Why should you care about increasing rigor in RTI and MTSS classrooms? There are two main reasons. First, the high school dropout rate is important. According to Bonnie Doren, Christopher Murray, and Jeff Gau

(2014), the most significant predictors of dropping out of school include a set of factors that can be changed. Individual factors include low grades; engagement in high-risk behavior; off-target parental expectations; and relationships with teachers and peers. How does this relate to the high school dropout rate of students with learning disabilities? Students with learning disabilities make up about 62% of secondary students with disabilities, and 21% of students with learning disabilities drop out of high school (Doren, Murray, & Gau, 2014).

Second, in today's society, students need to have a certain skillset for a job. The nonprofit National Association of Colleges and Employers surveyed hiring managers to determine the skills most desired from college graduates. Tied for first place were the ability to solve problems and the ability to make decisions (www.forbes.com/sites/susanadams/2014/11/12/the-10-skills-employers-most-want-in-2015-graduates/#5704f9142511). Similarly, *Leveling Up: How to Win in the Skills Economy* (www.payscale.com/data-packages/job-skills) noted that although 87% of recent graduates feel ready for the workplace, only 50% of the managers felt the same way about them. Managers call for graduates to obtain a high level of work-specific applicable skills as they transition to the workplace.

In addition to content and applicable skills, such as clear and accurate writing, speaking, and reasoning abilities, graduates should also have strong communication and problem-solving skills in order to succeed in postsecondary settings.

Dan Schawbel, research director at Future Workplace, said in a statement to Fast Company,

> No working day will be complete without writing an email or tackling a new challenge, so the sooner you develop these skills, the more employable you will become.
> (www.fastcompany.com/3059940/these-are-the-biggest-skills-that-new-graduates-lack, para. 7)

Although this research is focused on college graduates, all employers expect students to be able to think critically while making decisions.

A Brief History of RTI and MTSS

Multi-Tiered Systems of Supports (MTSS) are evolutionary and not revolutionary when it comes to identification of students with specific learning disabilities. When identifying students for learning disabilities and other special education services, all states at one point or another used an IQ–achievement discrepancy model. With this model, students are tested for their intelligence quotient (IQ), which is then compared to achievement measures of various academic areas. Though it was easy to determine score differences, there were some flaws in the system. The first flaw was that states chose different scores to reveal a discrepancy, such that a student might be eligible for services in one state but not another. In an increasingly transient culture, this is unacceptable. Another, even larger issue with the scores was the disagreement about what to do with students who had an academic need that did not satisfy the discrepancy. In many cases, students would be denied services and would not receive any substantial educational assistance for that academic year. The following year, those students would be even further behind, leading to a larger and sometimes significant discrepancy. So, the path to the extra help that services may provide would be to fail longer, thus giving rise to the attack on this approach as the "Wait to Fail" model.

This "Wait to Fail" approach has both a short- and long-term impact on students. In the short term, the student struggles for a longer time than necessary to receive help. In the long term, the effects can be even more devastating. By missing early learning principles and content, the student develops gaps in his or her learning that affect later development. For example, when a student lacks such academics as early number sense, that child will likely have problems with other math areas such as fractions and equations. Or, when a student does not acquire phonemic awareness skills early, this affects his or her later word attack skills and resulting comprehension.

MTSS and Significant Discrepancy

With the 2004 reauthorization of IDEA, Congress agreed,

There is no evidence that the IQ–achievement discrepancy formulas can be applied in a consistent and meaningful (reliable and valid) manner.

Moreover, schools were allowed and even encouraged to use an alternative process to determine whether a student could respond to scientifically research-validated interventions as part of the disabilities evaluation process, in what many researchers referred to as Response to Intervention (RTI). In contrast to the "Wait to Fail" model, RTI provides immediate and focused interventions when students are struggling in academics and/or have behavior or social-emotional concerns. The benefits can be seen at all grade levels.

A Word About RTI and MTSS

RTI and MTSS are often used synonymously. However, that doesn't need to be the case (Hurst, 2014). RTI is a Response to Intervention, meaning that the emphasis is on interventions in order to curb a student's lower performance. MTSS, or Multi-Tiered Systems of Supports, are generally aimed at different approaches designed to help students in different academic and behavioral situations. MTSS includes but is not limited to what is encompassed within an RTI program. Rather, MTSS is a broad approach, and its multiple tiers of support increase in intensity. Thus, the more intense the student's needs, the more intense the instruction and time for instruction and intervention.

MTSS includes multiple tiers of increasing intensity. At tier 1, instruction support is provided solely through the core education classroom. At tier 2, the student retains the support in the core classroom but receives additional supports on deficit areas during another time of the day. At tier 3, the supports in the core classroom remain but additional support is increased in time and intensity. Special education is additional support given beyond these tiers and different in approach.

MTSS Tiers

 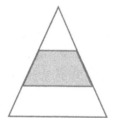  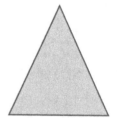

| Tier 1 services involve a teacher monitoring students' progress and adjusting to the students' needs. | Tier 2 services involve student progress monitoring and additional time devoted to curbing the deficit area. | Tier 3 services involve student progress monitoring and up to double the time devoted to curbing the deficit area. | Sparingly used non-diploma-track special education involves alternative standards. |

Both approaches can be implemented from the early childhood level through graduation, focus on content and behavior, include decision-making based on data and assessment, infuse research throughout the program, require collaboration among stakeholders, and require professional development. Additionally, RTI and MTSS include pinpointed interventions focused on students' areas of need, often called deficit areas.

Although there are distinct and important similarities, the differences define the purpose. Whereas an RTI system works to raise the achievement of the lowest performers through research-supported interventions, MTSS is designed to improve the education system as a whole. Through top-quality professional development, teachers and leaders learn research-supported instructional approaches aimed at student performance indicators. With an emphasis on prevention, core instruction is delivered using empirically validated approaches.

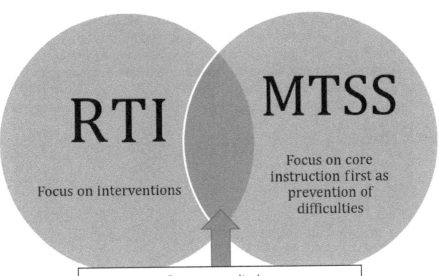

Rigor Through MTSS

Setting up a system of interventions that could lead to accurate iden-tification of learning disabilities is tricky. Movement among tiers must be well planned and requires the purposeful use of both formative and summative assessment. Additionally, teachers and leaders require training in intervention selection and implementation that is focused on specific student needs.

In this book, we focus on developing and improving the rigor of MTSS programs by focusing on programmatic needs, which include content selection, addressing the needs of students with academic weaknesses and strengths, developing prevention through effective core instruction, making informed instructional and intervention decisions, designing and implement-ing focused interventions, and using MTSS teams to further a school's plan and help more students.

Organization of This Book

In order to address both rigor and RTI/MTSS, we start in Chapter 1 by exploring the concept of rigor and how it relates to MTSS. Then, we move to describing tiered instruction and focusing on prevention and interven-tion in Chapters 2 and 3. In Chapters 4 and 5, we provide a wide range of rigorous evidence-based instructional strategies. We address assessment in Chapter 6, then shift our focus to behavior and social emotional learning (SEL) issues in Chapter 7. Finally, in Chapter 8, we look at the facets of a school-wide approach. After Chapter 1, the chapters are not sequential, so skip around as you need.

As you read the chapters, we hope you will find practical information that allows you to improve the effectiveness of your RTI/MTSS programs by enhancing the rigor.

1

Rigor and the RTI/MTSS Classroom

Rigor has been an area of increasing focus in education. However, when you talk with teachers and leaders, everyone seems to have a different understanding of what rigor means and, especially, what it looks like in the classroom. In this chapter, we look at why rigor is important, misconceptions related to rigor, a clear definition of rigor, and how rigor is incorporated in tiers 1, 2, and 3.

The Call for Rigor

In 1983, the National Commission on Excellence in Education released its landmark report *A Nation at Risk*. It painted a clear picture: Test scores were declining, lower standards resulted in American schools that were not competitive with schools from other countries, and students were leaving high school ill-prepared for the demands of the workforce.

Over 30 years later, similar criticisms are being leveled at today's schools.

New Calls for Rigor

Since *A Nation at Risk* was released, the call for more rigor has only increased. *The Condition of College and Career Readiness* (2011), a thorough report from the ACT, has reinforced high school graduates' lack of preparedness for college and for the workforce.

The focus on increased rigor has shifted to other grade ranges as well. For example, SREB's report *Preparing Middle Grades Students for*

High School Success (2008) underscores the need for rigor in the middle school years:

> Many students entering the ninth grade are not prepared for the more demanding course work required of high school students— and they know it. On a 2006 survey of more than 11,000 ninth-graders at *High Schools That Work* (HSTW) schools, 39 percent of students said they were not prepared with the necessary reading skills for college-preparatory high school courses. Additionally, 49 percent reported being unprepared in writing, 57 percent reported being unprepared in mathematics and 60 percent reported being unprepared in science.

(Bottoms & Timberlake, p. 1)

In 2010, the Common Core State Standards (www.corestandards.org) were created to increase the level of rigor in schools. Other recently revised state standards similarly reinforced the need. Rigor is at the center of these standards, and much of the push for new standards came from a concern about the lack of rigor in many schools today, as well as the need to prepare students for college and careers (Blackburn, 2012b).

Most recently, the Pew Research Center (2017) released information that the academic achievement of students in the United States lags behind that of students in many other countries (see Scores on the Programme for International Student Assessment). As Pew pointed out, "Recently released data from international math and science assessments indicate that U.S. students continue to rank around the middle of the pack, and behind many other advanced industrial nations" (www.pewresearch.org/fact-tank/2017/02/15/u-s-students-internationally-math-science/).

Scores on the Programme for International Student Assessment (PISA)		
Subject	*Ranking*	*Score Compared to Highest Score*
Reading	24 out of 71	497 compared to 535
Math	38 out of 71	470 compared to 564
Science	24 out of 71	496 compared to 556

The Need for Increased Rigor
for Students With Disabilities

According to the National Center for Special Education Research (Newman et al., 2011), 60% of young adults with disabilities reported having continued on to postsecondary education within eight years of leaving high school.

The National Center for Educational Statistics (U.S. Department of Education, 2016) found that, in 2013–2014, approximately 13% of college students had a disability and 4.5% of all college students had a learning disability (https://nces.ed.gov/fastfacts/display.asp?id=64).

Therefore, we must assess whether students with disabilities are appropriately prepared for college. The U.S. Department of Education's Office of Civil Rights discusses what students need to do to be successful in college. One item is of particular importance.

> Because all students will be expected to meet an institution's essential standards, students with disabilities need to take a high school curriculum that will prepare them to meet those standards. If students with disabilities plan to attend a rigorous postsecondary institution, they, like their peers without disabilities, need to make high school curriculum choices that support that goal.
>
> (www2.ed.gov/about/offices/list/
> ocr/transitionguide.html#keys)

When we look at these three pieces of information, the conclusion is clear: Students with disabilities need to be prepared for college, and rigor is an integral part of that.

Of the variety of reasons that rigor is important, which ones matter most to your students?

Key Shifts in the Standards

The Office of Vocational and Adult Education wanted to create a stronger link between adult education, postsecondary education, and work. To do so, it evaluated the Common Core State Standards, which had been created based on a broad range of research and with wide input from stakeholders. It then determined which of those essential skills were most relevant for post–high school plans. Finally, it shared the results in *Promoting College and Career-Ready Standards in Adult Basic Education*. First, let's look at three critical shifts that need to occur in schools in the areas of English/language arts and content literacy across the curriculum.

English/Language Arts and Literacy in History/Social Studies, Science, and Technical Subjects	
Texts Students Read and Questions for Writing and Speaking	
Shift	*Explanation*
Complexity: Regular practice with complex text and its academic language.	◆ Complexity of text that students are able to read is the greatest predictor of success in college and careers. ◆ Current gap in complexity between secondary texts and college/career texts is roughly four grade levels (Williamson, 2006).
Evidence: Reading, writing, and speaking grounded in evidence from text, both literary and informational.	◆ National assessment data and input from college faculty indicate that command of evidence is a key college and career readiness skill.
Knowledge: Building knowledge through content-rich nonfiction.	◆ Informational text makes up the vast majority of required reading in college and the workplace.

These shifts are critical for all students, including those with special needs. A teacher Barbara spoke with said, "My students can't even answer the questions. How am I supposed to ask them for evidence?" Requiring students to provide evidence for opinions and responses is a necessary skill that should start at the kindergarten level. It's simple. Just ask, "Why?" If they say that Clifford is a big dog, ask them, "Why?" If they explain that the main character in *Maniac Magee* by Jerry Spinelli did a particular action, ask, "Why?" When asking students to justify an antagonist's actions, ask, "Why?" Of course, with older students, we should use words such as *evidence* and *justification*, but the heart of citing evidence is answering *why*. These three shifts are not only important for students with special needs but they are also achievable. Next, there are also three key shifts related to mathematical thinking.

Mathematics	
Delving Deeply Into the Key Processes and Ideas Upon Which Mathematical Thinking Relies	
Shift	*Explanation*
Focus: Focusing strongly where the standards focus.	♦ Focusing deeply on the major work of each level will allow students to secure the mathematical foundations, conceptual understanding, procedural skill and fluency, and ability to apply the math they have learned to solve all kinds of problems— inside and outside the math classroom.
Coherence: Designing learning around coherent progressions from level to level.	♦ Create coherent progressions in the content within and across levels so that students can build new understanding onto previous foundations. That way, instructors can count on students having conceptual understanding of core content.
Rigor: Pursuing conceptual understanding, procedural skill and fluency, and application— all with equal intensity.	♦ Conceptual understanding of key concepts, procedural skill and fluency, and rigorous application of mathematics in real-world contexts.

Too often in mathematics, debates center on procedures or concepts. When answering a division of fractions problem, such as $\frac{1}{3} \div \frac{4}{5} = ?$, rather than only (a) understanding that four-fifths is larger than one-third so the answer will be less than 1 or (b) how to robotically invert and multiply, it is important for the student to understand both the reasoning and the procedures for dividing four-fifths into one-third. As such, the student may realize that equivalent fractions make better sense in this problem: $\frac{5}{15} \div \frac{12}{15} = ?$, equaling $\frac{5/12}{1}$ or $\frac{5}{12}$. Holding higher expectations for all students will have a profound impact on their long-term growth and development as seen through academic and behavioral performance.

Career Readiness Competencies

Finally, the National Association of Colleges and Employers (2017) has defined career readiness.

Career readiness is the attainment and demonstration of requisite competencies that broadly prepare college graduates for a successful transition into the workplace.

What are these requisite competencies? They are skills that are general and apply across all content areas, and are ones that are critical for student success in the workplace.

Career Readiness Competencies

Critical thinking/problem solving.
Oral/written communications.
Teamwork/collaboration.
Digital technology.
Leadership.
Professionalism/work ethic.
Career management.
Global/intercultural fluency.

Although these competencies are not necessarily measured on standardized achievement tests, they are important for students' long-term success. Many, such as a work ethic and the use of digital technology, are also integral to the learning process.

What parts of this information strike a chord with you? As you think about the competencies, do you believe your students can meet those standards?

Misconceptions About Rigor

Despite all the efforts to increase rigor in schools, there are seven commonly held misconceptions. Let's look at each.

Seven Misconceptions

Lots of homework is a sign of rigor.
Rigor means doing more.
Rigor is not for everyone.
Providing support means lessening rigor.
Resources equal rigor.
Standards alone take care of rigor.
Rigor is just one more thing to do.

Myth One: Lots of Homework Is a Sign of Rigor

For many people, the best indicator of rigor is the amount of homework required of students. Some teachers pride themselves on the amount of homework expected of their students, and there are parents who judge teachers by homework quantity. Realistically, all homework is not equally useful. Some of it is just busywork, assigned by teachers because principals or parents expect it. For some students, doing more homework in terms of quantity leads to burnout. When that occurs, students are less likely to complete homework and may be discouraged about any learning activity.

Myth Two: Rigor Means Doing More

"Doing more" often means doing more low-level activities, frequently repetitions of things already learned. Such narrow and rigid approaches to learning do not define a rigorous classroom. Students learn in many different ways. Just as instruction must vary to meet the individual needs of students, so must homework. Rigorous and challenging learning experiences will vary with the student. Their design will vary, as will their duration. Ultimately, it is the quality of the assignment that makes a difference in terms of rigor.

Myth Three: Rigor Is Not for Everyone

Often, teachers think that the only way to assure success for everyone is to lower standards and lessen rigor. This may mask a hidden belief that some students can't really learn at high levels. You may have heard of the Pygmalion effect—students live up to or down to our expectations of them. All students can complete rigorous work at high levels, whether they are advanced or have special needs. Does the end result look different for each of those students? Yes, but we know from our own experiences as teachers of struggling students reading far below their grade level that any teacher can be rigorous, and any student can reach higher levels with the right support.

Myth Four: Providing Support Means Lessening Rigor

In America, we believe in rugged individualism. We are to pull ourselves up by our bootstraps and do things on our own. Working in teams or accepting help is often seen as a sign of weakness. However, supporting students so that they can learn at high levels is central to the definition of rigor. As teachers design lessons that move students toward more challenging work, they must provide differentiated scaffolding to support them as they learn.

Myth Five: Resources Equal Rigor

We hear a common refrain from teachers: "If we buy this program, or textbook, or technology, then we would be rigorous." The right resources can certainly help increase the rigor in your classroom. However, raising the level of rigor for your students is not dependent on the resources you have. Think about the resources you have now. How can you use them more effectively? Do you use a textbook that includes true-false tests? Often, these are not rigorous because students can guess the answer. However, add one step for more rigor: Ask students to rewrite all false answers into true statements, and these tests now require students to demonstrate real understanding. It's not the resources; it's how you use them that make a difference.

Myth Six: Standards Alone Take Care of Rigor

Standards alone, even if they are rigorous, do not guarantee rigor in the classroom. The Common Core State Standards are designed to increase the level of rigor in classrooms across the nation. However, they were not designed to address instruction. In fact, they provide a framework for what is to be taught and what students are expected to know. If implemented without high levels of questioning or application, the Standards themselves are weakened. Your instructional practices, or how you implement standards, are just as critical as the curriculum.

Myth Seven: Rigor Is Just One More Thing to Do

Rigor is not another thing to add to your plate. Instead, rigor is increasing the level of expectation of what you are already doing. For example, if you are teaching vocabulary, instead of asking students to write their own definition of the word, ask them to write a riddle. It's the same end result but at higher levels.

Have you ever heard a teacher talk about rigor and use one of these seven misconceptions? Have you used one? How would you respond to that misconception now?

What Is Instructional Rigor?

Now, let's look at what rigor *is*. In *Rigor Is Not a Four-Letter Word* (2018), Barbara defines rigor as creating an environment in which . . .

◆ each student is expected to learn at high levels,
◆ each student is supported so he or she can learn at high levels, and.
◆ each student demonstrates learning at high levels.

Notice that we are looking at the environment you create in the classroom. The threefold approach to rigor is not limited to the curriculum that students are expected to learn. It is more than a specific lesson or instructional strategy. It is deeper than what a student says or does in response to a lesson. True rigor is the result of weaving together all elements of schooling to raise students to higher levels of learning. Let's take a deeper look at the three aspects of the definition.

Expectations

The first component of rigor is creating an environment in which each student is expected to learn at high levels. Having high expectations starts with the recognition that every student possesses the potential to succeed at his or her individual level. Almost every teacher or leader we talk with says, "We have high expectations for our students." Sometimes that is evidenced by the behaviors in the school; other times, however, faculty actions don't match the words. There are concrete ways to implement and assess rigor in classrooms. As you design lessons that incorporate more rigorous opportunities for learning, you will want to consider the questions that are embedded in the instruction. Higher level questioning is an integral part of a rigorous classroom. Look for open-ended questions at higher levels of critical thinking. It is also important to pay attention to how you respond to student questions. When we visit schools, it is not uncommon to see teachers who ask higher level questions. But for whatever reason, we then see some of the same teachers accept low-level responses from students. In rigorous classrooms, teachers push students to respond at high levels. They ask extending questions, or questions that encourage a student to explain their reasoning and think through ideas. When a student does not know the immediate answer but has sufficient background information to provide a response to the question, the teacher continues to probe and guide the student's thinking rather than moving on to the next student. Insist on thinking and problem solving.

High expectations are important, but the most rigorous schools assure that each student is supported so he or she can learn at high levels, which is the second part of our definition. It is essential that teachers design lessons that move students to more challenging work while simultaneously providing ongoing scaffolding to support students' learning as they move to those higher levels.

Scaffolding for Support

Providing additional scaffolding throughout lessons is one of the most important ways to support your students. Oftentimes, students have the ability or knowledge to accomplish a task but are overwhelmed by the complexity of it, and they get lost in the process. This can occur in a variety of ways, but it requires that teachers ask themselves during every step of their lessons, "What extra support might my students need?"

Examples of Scaffolding Strategies

- ◆ Asking guiding questions.
- ◆ Chunking information.
- ◆ Highlighting or color-coding steps in a project.
- ◆ Writing standards as questions for students to answer.

◆ Using visuals and graphic organizers, such as a math graphic organizer for word problems, maps to accompany history lessons, or color-coded paragraphs to help students make meaning of texts.

Demonstration of Learning

The third component of a rigorous classroom is providing each student with opportunities to demonstrate learning at high levels. There are two aspects of students' demonstration of learning. First, we need to provide rigorous tasks and assignments for students. What we've learned is that if we want students to show that they understand what they learned at a high level, we also need to provide opportunities for students to demonstrate they have truly mastered that learning at more than a basic lesson. Many teachers use Bloom's Taxonomy or Webb's Depth of Knowledge (DOK; Level 3 or above is rigorous). We prefer Webb's DOK for a more accurate view of the depth and complexity of rigor (see Examples of Guidelines for Rigor for Bloom's Taxonomy and Webb's Depth of Knowledge), and we'll explain that more fully in Chapter 3.

Examples of Guidelines for Rigor for Bloom's Taxonomy and Webb's Depth of Knowledge	
Bloom's Taxonomy	*Webb's DOK Level 3*
Analyzing Evaluating Creating *Note:* Although the verbs are important, you must pay attention to what comes after the verb to determine rigor.	Does the assessment focus on deeper knowledge? Are students proposing and evaluating solutions or recognizing and explaining misconceptions? Do students go beyond the text information while demonstrating that they understand the text? Do students support their ideas with evidence? Does the assessment require reasoning, planning, using evidence, and a higher level of thinking than the previous two levels (such as a deeper level of inferencing)?

Second, in order for students to demonstrate their learning, they must first be engaged in academic tasks—precisely, those in the classroom. In too many classrooms, most of the instruction consists of teacher-centered large-group instruction, perhaps in an interactive lecture or discussion format. The general practice during these lessons is for the teacher to ask a question and then call on a student to respond. This provides an opportunity for one student to demonstrate understanding, but the remaining students don't do so. Another option would be for the teacher to allow all students to pair-share, respond with thumbs up or down, write their answers on small whiteboards and share their responses, or respond on handheld computers that tally the responses. Such activities hold each student accountable for demonstrating his or her understanding.

How does this explanation inform your understanding of rigor?

Rigor in the Tiers

Rigor is important in all tiers. It can be easy to forget that the focus of MTSS is on the core instruction, or tier 1. Tiers 2 and 3 are designed to support the core instruction at increasingly intense levels. All too often, students receiving interventions in RTI or MTSS model are labeled based on the most intensive intervention level they are receiving. For example, a student receiving tiered services for reading comprehension may erroneously be called a *tier 2 student*. Rather than letting intervention levels dictate the placement of the student, is important to recognize that every student in an MTSS model should be a *tier 1 student*. The reason is based on the definition of the MTSS model itself. If a student were in tier 3, then that student is also in tier 1 and could therefore be viewed as a tier 1 student. If a label were needed in order to identify what level of intervention is being implemented, then it may be more appropriate to call the student a *tier 1–3 student*. This signification is more than avoiding a negative connotation; it is a more accurate portrayal of the instruction and intervention being provided. Also, it emphasizes that the student is still receiving core instruction and thus is on a diploma track.

Rigor at Each Tier

Each element of rigor should be reflected at all three tiers.

Element	Tier 1	Tier 2	Tier 3
Expectations	High expectations, the same as other students who do not have disabilities.	High expectations for general education standards, with understanding that meeting them requires additional support.	High expectations for general education standards, with understanding that meeting them requires more intensive support.
Support	Progress monitoring drives support differentiated as needed to meet student's need.	Progress monitoring with scaffolding and support dedicated to curbing deficit areas.	Progress monitoring with increased amounts of time dedicated to curbing deficit areas.
Demonstration of Learning	Students expected to demonstrate understanding of the general education standards.	Students expected to demonstrate understanding of the general education standards, although it may take more time or an alternative assessment.	Students expected to demonstrate understanding of the general education standards, although it may take more time or an alternative assessment.

Conclusion

The need to increase rigor in our schools, including in our MTSS programs, is critical if we want to appropriately prepare our students for life after high school, whether that is a postsecondary college, the military, or going directly into the workforce. Rigor, however, is more than simply making things harder for students. It is a weaving together of high expectations, scaffolding and support, and demonstration of learning. By holding our students with special needs to high standards and by providing them the right support, we can ensure that they will be successful.

2

Tiered Instruction

Introduction

Multi-Tiered Systems of Supports (MTSS) are primarily designed to improve academic and social emotional performance. At times, MTSS is used only through interventions targeted at deficit areas for our most struggling students. Many of those students are identified as having a learning disability. Although focusing on students who struggle will likely improve an overall school score because it brings up the bottom numbers, it doesn't necessarily improve the scores of average or higher achieving students. MTSS is not a replacement for special education; rather, it is a curriculum and instruction model designed to improve *all* students' performance, which includes raising the level of rigor. This means that the MTSS model must consider the needs of students with disabilities, students with academic struggles, students meeting expectations, students outperforming expectations, and even students labeled as gifted. In other words, MTSS is designed to be an approach that benefits all students.

Although the goal of MTSS is to improve core instruction, increase rigor for all students, and help provide effective differentiation for students in order to improve academic performance, MTSS will not replace or eliminate special education and should not be used to hinder the process of identifying students who need services. MTSS teams should work with special education to ensure this.

The Tiers

At the core of MTSS are the tiers of instruction.

In a multi-tier model, all students are held to rigorous expectations, but they receive different and varying levels of student assistance. There are similarities between special education and how differentiation is assigned

| Tier 3: Individualized |
| Tier 2: Small Group |
| Tier 1: Whole Class, General, Nonspecific, UDL |

in tiered interventions. For students who have already been identified with a disability, student assistance at the individual level should be apparent across all tiers. Having an MTSS model should never be a reason to undermine the benefits or legal requirements granted with special education. What remains a question with special education, however, is the placement where the services will be provided. Students with disabilities must always be taught in the least restrictive environment.

In tier 1, or core instruction, students receive assistance or differentiation; however, these supports are general, nonspecific, or designed for whole-group implementation. Although many teachers believe that they must differentiate through individualizing instruction, that isn't always practical. In fact, individualization of instruction is quite complex, especially in a large class setting. Instead, while teaching rigorous standards, teachers differentiate through general ideas and whole-class adjustments.

Interventions are increased in tiers 2 and 3. In tier 2, the teacher works with small groups of students, and student assistance is often set by the needs of the small group. The amount of time for tier 2 support is typically between 30 and 45 minutes per day.

In tier 3, the teacher usually works one-on-one with a student, although there are times this occurs in small groups. Student assistance is designed to meet the specific needs of the student receiving the intervention. Tier 3 support is typically between 45 and 60 minutes per day.

Diagnosis and Assessment of Students With Learning Disabilities

A specific learning disability is defined as:

a disorder in one or more of the basic psychological processes involved in understanding or in using language, spoken or written, that may manifest itself in the imperfect ability to listen, think, speak, read, write, spell or do mathematical calculations, including conditions such as perceptual disabilities, brain injury, minimal brain dysfunction, dyslexia, and developmental aphasia.

(Individuals with Disabilities Education Act (IDEA), 2004 , p. 118)

This means that the student has a difficulty learning that results in an academic deficiency.

Possible Academic Deficiency Areas

Oral expression.
Listening comprehension.
Written expression.
Basic reading skill.
Reading fluency skills.
Reading comprehension.
Mathematical computation.
Mathematics problem solving.

These deficiencies impact all content areas and social emotional learning. For example, a student with a listening comprehension deficit will likely struggle in social studies, in the arts, mathematics (particularly with vocabulary, verbal reasoning, and word problem solving), and even social exchanges with peers and adults unless empirically validated interventions are implemented. Even then, difficulties may remain and can negatively affect students' reaching high levels of rigor. As such, interventions must be based on assessment, carefully planned and accurately executed with fidelity.

Multi-Tier Models

In a multi-tier model (MTSS or RTI), an education team uses accurate assessment and implementation of empirically validated instruction intervention to inform a student's evaluation for learning disabilities. When students do not respond well to research-based core instruction alone, a school team may decide to provide tier 2 interventions to help that student achieve. If, however, the student does not achieve in core and tier 2 intervention, then that student may be selected for tier 3 intervention. If, even after these intense levels of assistance, the student does not show improved achievement, then the student may be evaluated for special education services.

This approach may be used along with the significant discrepancy model to determine who needs special education services in order to achieve. However, the MTSS or RTI approach does not negate the need for alternative evaluation for special education eligibility.

Wisconsin regulations are specific. After a student has been identified with possible deficiencies, he or she may only be found to have an impairment of specific learning disabilities if the individualized education program (IEP) team has sufficient data that shows the following characteristics:

1. The student demonstrates insufficient progress in one or more of eight academic areas. In determining "insufficient progress," IEP teams must consider data from progress monitoring following intensive general education interventions.
2. The student demonstrates inadequate classroom (academic) achievement, using a valid and reliable standardized achievement test administered following intensive general education interventions.
3. The student's insufficient progress and inadequate classroom achievement are not primarily caused by one or more exclusionary factors, such as limited English proficiency or whether the student received appropriate general education instruction in the area(s) of concern.

Implementing a comprehensive data-based approach potentially provides more accurate, efficient, and effective information in making a disabilities determination. Also, having such a system in place implies that all students receive high-quality instruction with accurate assessment and collaborative teacher planning on scope and sequence and progressions that will further strengthen core instruction. This approach will also reduce the number of students who are inappropriately referred for special education evaluation. If implemented correctly, this approach may provide other benefits such as increased overall student performance in academic content and decreased numbers of students who are currently enrolled in special education services (www.wisconsinrticenter.org/assets/files/RtI-SLD-Brief-2014.pdf).

What did you learn about determining the tiers for students?

How do you differ your tiers of instruction and intervention for struggling students?

Progress Monitoring

Screening should be done at least twice a year. At a minimum, after each screening the MTSS team should review students' scores in order to determine who was performing within the expected range, below expectations, significantly below expectations, higher than expectations, and significantly higher than expectations. For students scoring below expectations and for students who are identified by teachers as having difficulties, it is particularly important to monitor the progress between screenings. Monitoring the progress of a student receiving intervention gives the MTSS team a clearer picture of that student's progress toward both the intervention and performance in core instruction. Monitoring the progress of students scoring within the expected range but whom teachers have identified as struggling is important for predicting future low scores on the screener. Low growth on a progress monitoring test could be used to place a student in an intervention. This way, the student does not have to wait until screening in order to receive help.

Universal Design for Learning

Earlier, we pointed out the importance of differentiated instruction. One model for differentiation is Universal Design for Learning (UDL). UDL pushes for differentiation and against a one-for-all instruction and curriculum approach. However, UDL isn't about strict individualization; rather, it's about providing multiple ways for students to access content and about revealing understanding for students. The National Center on UDL (www.udlcenter. org) identified three central guidelines for implementing UDL: (a) multiple means of engagement, (b) multiple means of representation, and (c) multiple means of action and expression.

Overview of Universal Design for Learning		
Provide Multiple Means of Representation	**Provide Multiple Means of Action and Expression**	**Provide Multiple Means of Engagement**
Provide options for perception.	Provide options for physical action.	Provide options for recruiting interest.
Provide options for language and symbols.	Provide options for expressive skills and fluency.	Provide options for sustaining effort and persistence.
Provide visual, such as graphic organizers, to aid comprehension.	Provide options for executive functions.	Provide options for self-regulation.

We will go into more detail on each of these in Chapter 3, when we discuss the tiers in depth. However, at this point, we provide a quick look at each of these areas.

Provide Multiple Means of Representation

Using multiple representations for instruction has been supported in research for nearly 100 years. In 1925, Samuel Orton investigated why some students had difficulty with language. He learned that even though many students had average or above-average intelligence, they still struggled with reading, and he determined that he could help these students by matching kinesthetic, auditory, and visual sensory input with literacy. He later teamed up with Anna Gillingham to develop what we now know as the Orton-Gillingham reading program. Because of the popularity of this program and its effectiveness for students with disabilities, other programs have followed based on the same multisensory language approach. Mathematics has also seen an increase in the use of multisensory approaches.

One such method is the concrete to representational to abstract sequence of instruction, proven effective for students learning basic facts, fractions and decimals computation, and algebraic equations solving. As a central guideline for UDL, the use of representations does not need to be relegated to students in intervention or special education settings. Rather, graphic organizers, concrete manipulatives, video modeling, color-coding, and other means of representation should be made available to all students. However, the use of these representations may be differentiated based on students' needs.

For example, in her 10th-grade English class, Mrs. Carter likes to show the movie *To Kill a Mockingbird* before students read the book. It provides a visualization of key characters, the setting, and some contextualized pieces for students who struggle with reading. She has found that students who see the movie first are better able to connect what they read with what they witnessed. However, Mrs. Carter does not show the movie first in her ninth-grade Honors English class; she has the students read the book first and then watch the movie. She states that this approach lets for students analyze the differences between the movie and the book as they understood it. She even lets her students choose current actors who would better represent the characters based on how they viewed them.

Provide Multiple Means of Action and Expression

The use of action and expression within lessons enhances engagement, which we will discuss in the next section. It also allows for better access to content. Student movement must be purposeful and plentiful as part of the lesson. A teacher who uses movement to connect to phonemes likely helps students remember letter sounds. In one classroom, Ms. Helmick has students form a *b* in their left hand and pretend to bounce the ball while saying the letter sound /b/. To differentiate that from the letter *d*, the students form a *d* in their right hand and click their wrist downward, like a dog eating from a dish, while saying the letter sound /d/. In this example, Ms. Helmick is not only using movement to support learning phonemes but is also having students verbally practice. Every student should speak every day about every subject discussed. Getting the students to express their learning improves the opportunity for input, retention, and recall. As students show success, the amount of action and expression may be gradually reduced or faded to help students with generalization.

Provide Multiple Means of Engagement

Engagement means having students actively involved in the lesson. However, engagement alone does not make a lesson effective. Students should be engaged in content-focused instruction that meets rigorous standards and helps them grow academically. Therefore, instead of simply looking to engage students, it is important to increase students' academic learning time, which occurs by adding tier 2 or 3 interventions.

Engagement is enhanced when students are motivated to learn. There are two components of intrinsic motivation, both of which are addressed in the engagement portion of UDL. First, UDL recommends that we attempt to meet students' interests, as the first component of intrinsic motivation is value. In other words, students are more motivated when they see relevance in a lesson. For some students, this may mean understanding that skateboarding is linked to geometry; for younger students, this may mean seeing their names in a word problem.

The second part of intrinsic motivation is success. Students are more motivated when they are successful or when they believe they can be successful. It is therefore critical that we provide an appropriate amount of challenge and balance that with support, as recommended in UDL. In other words, we need to provide rigorous instruction but also provide appropriate scaffolding that allows students to be successful.

These three essential elements of UDL help support student success in both core instruction and tiered intervention. However, these elements are relative terms and should not be used in isolation or without incorporating other effective approaches, such as explicit and systematic instruction. Additionally, each of the elements could be augmented through technology.

What aspects of UDL do you think you need to enhance in your classroom or program? Why?

Overall Components for Effective Implementation

There are also components that should be implemented at the school level for a successful MTSS program. Oregon's Response to Instruction and Intervention (ORTII, 2016) lists nine essential components for successful implementation of an MTSS framework.

Nine Components for Effective Implementation

1. School culture.
2. Leadership.
3. Professional learning.
4. Teaming and data-based decision-making.
5. Research-based core curriculum and effective instructional practices.
6. Universal screening.
7. Research-based interventions.
8. Progress monitoring.
9. Specific learning disability (SLD) identification using an RTI framework.

Using Oregon's framework, let's look at the details within an MTSS approach.

School Culture

> Core teachers are integral to student performance, thus integral to MTSS in general.
>
> —Todd Wiedemann, Assistant Director
> of Kansas MTSS (2016)

Developing a school culture requires belief not just in the students but in the teachers as well. Teachers are the most important part of a school. Teachers not only instruct but also develop curriculum, collaborate and consult with parents, counsel, coach, nurse, and entertain. With such a breadth of duties for classroom teachers, it is essential to focus on key components of instruction and performance outcomes as a goal. As the following figure shows, the school MTSS goals—this set is in literacy—are displayed in the teachers'

Priority skills	Sound identification	Blending and segmenting card 5 and 6	Long and short vowels	Vowels in every syllable	Fluency (prosody)	Multisyllabic words
Instructional strategy	Skill groups assigned by teachers	Provides extra practice based on accuracy of student response.	More than one opportunity to practice each new skill "vowel warm-ups"	Promptly corrects errors with provision of correct model	Teacher demonstrates the task	Provides opportunities for practice after each step in instruction
Active engagement or behavior management strategy	Limit/reduce transition time (use songs during transitions)	Choral responses	Action responses: Touching and pointing on vowel warm-ups	Choral response	Choral, partner and individual fluent reading	Choral responses

workroom. They are emphasizing what skills to prioritize, strategies per skill, and how to keep students active during instruction.

Leadership

Leadership is key to the success of MTSS. When listing the largest barriers to effective MTSS implementation, Todd Wiedemann, Assistant Director of Kansas MTSS (2016), included personnel and leadership engagement. The North Carolina MTSS Leadership Team (2016) agreed, stating, "Leadership and shared responsibility is a critical component of MTSS in North Carolina." The team further stated that leadership should be at both the school and district levels and should include administrators, representative teachers and staff, and even community leaders and families.

When making a change as large as MTSS, both district- and school-level leadership must have a clear vision and dedication to the change so that it benefits every student. MTSS is much more than adding interventions to grade-level teams. Leaders must present a commitment to the use of data for altering core instruction and designing focused interventions for students who are struggling. Through such leadership, the entire staff will own the process.

Professional Learning

Each state we contacted in the development of this book pointed to the need for focused and high-quality professional development. Professional development is likely needed for several aspects of MTSS, including but not limited to data analysis, core instruction, formative assessment development, and intervention delivery. In her doctoral research, Barbara found there are seven characteristics of effective professional development (Blackburn, 2000).

Key Elements of Effective Staff Development

Clear purpose linked to research, student data, goals, and needs.
Accountability through classroom use of ideas and impact on students.
Development of a common, shared language.
Shared decision-making that includes an emphasis on teacher input.
Incorporation of relevant, practical, hands-on activities.
Integration of opportunities for follow-up and application.
Strong leadership and a positive, collegial atmosphere.

With professional development, educators must be afforded access to empirically validated practices. Content must be emphasized (Heller, Daehler, Wong, Shinohara, & Miratrix, 2012), and examples must be shown through modeling of lessons. This may happen through job coaching or through instructional videos.

Other aspects to be considered are that sustained professional development over several months with job-embedded skills is likely to improve practices. It is best to focus on empirically validated practices and not short-term enjoyment or what is the most fun. While entertainment is preferable, quality instruction does not need to be "fun" but rather informative, inspiring, and geared to improve student performance. The effectiveness of MTSS, much like several other programs, is tied to sustained, accurate, and focused professional development.

Teaming and Data-Based Decision-Making

When it comes to the data, teacher collaboration is imperative. Student achievement is a shared responsibility among all staff, administrators and teachers alike. In a study measuring the impact of collaboration on student achievement, Ronfeldt, Farmer, McQueen, and Grissom (2015) found that schools with better collaborative efforts have higher achievement in math and reading.

Data-based decision-making is central to MTSS at all levels of instruction and intervention (www.rti4success.org/essential-components-rti/data-based-decision-making). The use of screening measures, progress monitoring, diagnostics, and additional formative assessments allows data teams to make informed decisions regarding instructional approaches, intervention selection, student placement per tier, and even disability identification, when appropriate per state law.

Research-Based Core Curriculum and Effective Instructional Practices

The North Carolina MTSS Leadership Team (2016) shared, "Logistically, a school does not possess the resources to compensate for poorly implemented core instruction with supplemental interventions." Effective instruction is based on the needs of the students. Witzel and Little (2016) argued that when aligning research to a school's needs, it is important to take into consideration the interaction effects between four components.

Four Components

a. Assessment requirements and outcomes
    i. Summative
    ii. Formative.
b. Learner characteristics
    i. Working memory
    ii. Attention
    iii. Executive functioning
    iv. Interest level.
c. Curriculum requirements and choices
    i. Standards
    ii. Textbooks
    iii. Teacher autonomy
    iv. Intervention content.
d. Instructional decisions
    i. Explicit and systematic
    ii. Project-based additions
    iii. Visual representations.

Too often, we attend a training on the "latest and greatest" approach. Sometimes, the presenter even presents research. However, on a closer look, the research isn't rigorous, isn't generalizable, or may not even resemble the population we teach. In several cases, the research presented isn't even based on academic performance but was validated based on student self-efficacy. Although motivation is integral, increasing student performance is the primary need when deciding on effective practices.

Universal Screening

Universal screening should be conducted with every student at least twice a year in an effort to identify or predict which students may be struggling or even exceeding academically. Screening should provide an accurate view of who is achieving, predict students' future achievement, be quick to deliver, and be validated to match statewide outcomes assessments, such as end-of-year or end-of-course exams.

Research-Based Interventions

Intervention research has similarities and differences from core research. As with research on core instruction, it is important to take into account details on the research per each deficit skill improvement. Student population and research methodology must be considered. However, student population labels require some lenience. Although there is a difference between students with academic difficulties and students with disabilities, much of the research on building deficit skills combines students with and without disabilities. Therefore, we need to look across both populations when reviewing intervention research.

Progress Monitoring

Whereas universal screening provides a general look at who is struggling or succeeding, progress monitoring determines students' rate of learning or improvement. It is important to monitor the progress of students identified with academic struggles to determine whether they are improving at an appropriate rate. During interventions, progress monitoring enables a team to determine the effectiveness of the intervention. In addition, it is important to assess students' progress in the core. Such benchmark assessments allow the data team to determine whether or not the intervention is having an effect on core or tier 1 performance.

Specific Learning Disabilities Identification Using MTSS Framework

School districts now use MTSS approaches to determine whether a student has a specific learning disability (SLD). Because MTSS is focused on addressing deficit skills, both academic and behavioral, it is most effective and efficient to start early. The longer a student waits to receive help, the more likely it is that problems become complex and thus more difficult to remediate.

According to the reauthorized Individuals with Disabilities Education Improvement Act (2004), 34 C.F.R. §300.07, districts

1) Must not require the use of severe discrepancy between intellectual ability and achievement for determining whether a child has a specific learning disability as defined in §300.8 (c)(10);

2) Must permit the use of a process based on the child's response to scientific, research-based intervention; and

3) May permit the use of other alternative research-based procedures for determining whether a child has a specific learning disability as defined in §300.8 (c)(10).

In 2011, 94% of schools reported implementing some degree of RTI/MTSS, and 66% of schools reported using RTI/MTSS as a part of the process for determining eligibility for special education (Cortiella & Horowitz, 2014; Moore, Sabousky, & Witzel, 2017).

Which of the nine components do you think are implemented effectively in your school? Which need improvement?

Conclusion

The heart of MTSS is meeting all students' needs through multiple levels and intensities of instruction. The various tiers do not lower expectations for students; all students are held to rigorous standards. However, students are provided differing levels of support in each tier. Assessment, through both diagnosis and progress monitoring, is also a part of an effective MTSS program and ensures that the needs of students with learning disabilities are met. Finally, there are overall school components that are critical for successful implementation of an effective, rigorous MTSS program.

3

Prevention,
Then Intervention

At the heart of every successful MTSS is a focus on improved tier 1 or core instruction before moving to specialized intervention strategies. When a school culture emphasizes best practices and rigor for all there will likely be high student performance. Oftentimes, we have focused so much on students' deficits, that it is counterproductive. As one teacher told Barbara, "There's just so much wrong with my students, I can't do anything about it." When we only focus on deficits, we tend to lower our expectations, and thus, the level of rigor.

Prevention: Tier 1

Ken Howell noted that in MTSS, there is a shift in thinking: "The central question is not 'What about the students is causing the performance discrepancy?' but rather 'What about the interaction of the curriculum, instruction, learners, and learning environment should be altered so that the students will learn?'" (Dorman, Wheeler, & Diamond, 2010, p. 1).

There is a sharp difference in these two comments. One focuses on what the student is doing wrong, and one focuses on what we can adjust to help him or her improve. In tier 1, we are saying that we will start with the highest expectations and do what we can to help students be successful. Then, if that doesn't work, we'll move to more intensive options.

This is reflective of a rigorous culture. Rigor is not setting a student up for failure; it is saying, "We are going to expect the best and do what we can to help him or her meet those expectations." Older deficit models have a different approach: start with what students cannot do and hope they will improve. In tier 1, we plan for the prevention of deficits before we use interventions. This does not mean that students with SLD will be ignored; rather, we provide the best possible core instruction before moving to tier 2. Additionally, improved core instruction benefits all students at all levels of performance.

Rigorous Expectations Within Core Content

Core Beliefs

When it comes to instruction, there is no one set of procedures or models that works for all students in all situations. However, there are at least five core principles that drive student learning outcomes.

Core Principles

1. All students can learn at rigorous levels.
2. Students must be engaged in order to learn.
3. Standards are the floor and not the ceiling.
4. Students deserve empirically validated practices.
5. Data can be used to drive instructional decision-making.

Note: Each of these principles should be included, but this should not be viewed as an all-inclusive list.

---

1. All Students Can Learn at Rigorous Levels

Although every teacher believes that all students can learn, there are some circumstances when a student falls behind quickly, making it difficult to catch up. In such cases, some people may be quick to refer the student to special education, but there may be reasons why the student should not be in special education. Moreover, there may be more appropriate and even quicker actions that can be taken. To believe that all students can learn requires a teacher to believe that all students can learn in her or his room. This may require doing things differently than before, from changing a class environment to altering seating structures to even creating multiple lessons to be taught concurrently. It is important for teachers to recognize their extreme power to help turn around a student's academic career and his or her future.

Believing that all students can learn at high levels means having high expectations for each student, which is a critical aspect of rigor. Robert Marzano and Michael Toth (2014) compared teachers who had high expectations and low expectations of students. Their findings are interesting. They discovered that teachers behave in different ways when they have high or low expectations of their students. For example, Tomazz is a bright student. He always turns in his homework, is the first to raise his hand to answer a question, asks questions that enhance the content, and makes straight A's.

Libby, on the other hand, struggles. She never turns in her homework, is always a step behind, never raises her hand in class, and if called on, she mumbles an answer so no one can hear her.

Let's assume that at the beginning of the year, you start out with high expectations for both Tomazz and Libby. Over the first few weeks, your expectations for Tomazz go up as he continues to thrive. For Libby, perhaps at a subconscious level, your expectations go down. You may even think something like, "Well, she's doing the best she can, bless her heart."

Marzano and Toth found that we then begin to treat the two of them differently. For Tomazz, we ask higher order questions. Libby gets basic recall questions. Of course differentiating questions is important, but both students deserve to be pushed. So, if you are going to ask, "What color is the dog?" then at least ask why she knows that. We give Tomazz more wait time because we know he will come up with the answer. We stand closer to him, give him more eye contact, and use more positive language. None of those are true with Libby. Over time, Libby becomes more withdrawn, and it becomes a vicious cycle.

We may say that we believe all children can learn, but our actions do not always reflect that sentiment. Our words also reflect our beliefs and expectations. For example, when we say, "Oh, he's from *that* neighborhood" or "She's in Special Ed, that's why she's not learning," we are showing our belief that not all students can learn. Paying attention to our words and actions is critical when it comes to holding students to rigorous standards.

Have you ever demonstrated your low expectations of a student? What happened?

2. Students Must Be Engaged in Order to Learn

Being engaged in a school environment means that students must have appropriate academic behavior established and be motivated to learn. Although many students come to school ready to learn, others do not. In some cases, we must take care of primary needs before we can focus on academic ones. It is obvious that a child who is hungry or unloved would struggle in school more than one who is nourished and cared for.

Central to engagement is academic learning time. Academic learning time is the efficiency and appropriateness of the lessons taught. As stated by the North Carolina MTSS Leadership Team (2016),

MTSS is about access and equitable educational experiences for all students. All students deserve and benefit from opportunities to engage in rigorous instruction within a diverse setting of learners.

Characteristics of Engagement

Eric Jenson (2013) pointed out four components that are present during student engagement:

1. The engaged student pays attention in the sense that he or she focuses on the tasks associated with the work being done.
2. The engaged student is committed. He or she voluntarily uses the resources under his or her control, such as time, attention, and effort, to support the activity.
3. The engaged student is persistent, sticking with the task despite difficulties.
4. The engaged student finds meaning and value in the task.

Carolyn Chapman and Nicole Vagle, in their book *Motivating Students: 25 Strategies to Light the Fire of Engagement* (2011), provided more specific information to describe engaged students. You can use the table below, which describes how students feel and what they do, as a checklist to determine your students' level of engagement.

A Motivating, Engaging Classroom	
How Do Students Feel?	*What Are Students Doing?*
Excited	Problem solving
Respected	Processing
Challenged	Questioning
Stimulated	Discussing
Enthusiastic	Sharing
Content	Cooperating
Accepted	Collaborating
Energetic	Being engaged
Safe	Planning
Positive	Producing
Upbeat	Learning
Cooperative	Showing evidence of learning
Confident	Thinking
Hopeful	Discussing, asking questions, and posing solutions to problems
	Making links and connections to their learning
	Being metacognitive, reflecting on their learning, and setting goals for their next steps

Source: Reprinted from *Motivating Students: 25 Strategies to Light the Fire of Engagement* by Carolyn Chapman and Nicole Vagle.

In each of the preceding descriptions of engagement, everything is student-focused. You may be wondering if you can make a difference with student engagement. John Hattie in *Visible Learning* (2008) pointed out that over 50% of students' academic outcomes result from what the teacher does in the classroom.

For example, let's examine four typical behaviors you commonly see in the classroom. Struggling students may be engaged, detached, bored, or anxious. What specific steps can you take in each case to improve student engagement?

Typical Behaviors		
Characteristic	*What You See*	*What to Do*
Engaged	Is involved and focused on learning.	Monitor periodically and adjust if needed.
Detached	Withdraws from lesson.	Provide specific small steps and a strategy that requires involvement to get them started.
Bored	Exhibits off-task behavior.	Provide more challenge or relevance.
Anxious	Exhibits agitation or off-task behavior.	Provide more support and coaching.

Engaging students at high levels is critical to student success in a rigorous MTSS classroom.

3. Standards Are the Floor and Not the Ceiling

We usually assume that our state standards are rigorous. They can be, but oftentimes they can be taught in non-rigorous ways. Therefore, we should use the standards as a starting point and enhance them with a framework for high levels of thinking.

Bloom's Taxonomy

Probably the most popular tool used to determine high expectations is Bloom's Taxonomy.

Levels of Bloom's Taxonomy

Remember.
Understand.
Apply.
Analyze.
Evaluate.
Create.

Bloom's may be a good starting point, but there is also a challenge with this approach. Most teachers have come to associate Bloom's levels with specific verbs. However, verbs can be deceptive. For example, on the taxonomy, *create* is at the highest level. But is that always true? When conducting walkthroughs in a school, we observed a lesson in which students were creating get-well cards for a sick classmate. Is that rigorous? Of course not. The verb is deceptive.

Let's look at another example: After studying Greek and Roman civilizations, students create three-dimensional models to compare and contrast the two civilizations using only edible material.

Is that assignment rigorous? Students are asked to design a creative way to present their information. It seems challenging. After all, they have to be creative to complete the project. But if we take away the creative aspect, students are basically recalling information, which is at a low level of Bloom's. We believe that it's important to provide opportunities for students to demonstrate their creative sides, but don't assume that is rigorous.

Webb's Depth of Knowledge

Although Bloom's is widely used, we prefer using Webb's Depth of Knowledge (DOK) as a benchmark of rigor. Webb's DOK has four levels focusing on depth and complexity.

Webb's Depth of Knowledge

Level 1: Recall.
Level 2: Skill/Concept.
Level 3: Strategic Thinking.
Level 4: Extended Thinking.

As a side note, there is a very popular diagram of DOK verbs on the internet. A wheel or circle is divided into quarters, and each section lists verbs for that level. Simplifying the DOK to verbs takes us back to the same problem as with Bloom's: verbs can be deceptive.

When Barbara was writing *Rigor in Your Classroom: A Toolkit for Teachers* (2014), she contacted Webb's office to ask to reprint the wheel in her book. She received a quick and clear response: Webb did not create the DOK verb wheel, does not endorse it, and does not believe it represents the four dimensions. We understand why. The DOK levels are descriptors of depth and complexity that go far beyond simplistic verbs.

For example, take a look at the full description of the four levels for math.

Summary Definitions of DOK for Math			
Level 1	*Level 2*	*Level 3*	*Level 4*
Requires students to recall or observe facts, definitions, and terms. Includes simple one-step procedures. Includes computing simple algorithms (e.g., sum, quotient). *Examples:* Recall or recognize a fact, term, or property. Represent in words, pictures, or symbols a math object or relationship. Perform a routine procedure, such as measuring.	Requires students to make decisions on how to approach a problem. Requires students to compare, classify, organize, estimate, or order data. Often involves procedures with two or more steps. *Examples:* Specify and explain relationships between facts, terms, properties, or operations.	Requires reasoning, planning, or use of evidence to solve a problem or algorithm. May involve an activity with more than one possible answer. Requires conjecture or restructuring of problems. Involves drawing conclusions from observations, citing evidence and developing logical arguments for concepts. Uses concepts to solve non-routine problems.	Requires complexity at least at the level of DOK 3 but also an extended time to complete the task. A project that requires extended time but repetitive or lower-DOK tasks is not at Level 4. Requires complex reasoning, planning, developing, and thinking. May require students to make several connections and apply one approach among many to solve the problem. May involve complex restructuring of data, establishing and evaluating criteria to solve problems.

(Continued)

(Continued)

| At higher grades, solve a quadratic equation or a system of two linear equations with two unknowns. | Select procedure according to criteria and perform it. Use concepts to solve routine multiple-step problems. | *Examples:* Formulate original problem, given situation. Formulate mathematical model for complex situation. Produce a sound and valid mathematical argument. Devise an original proof. Critique a mathematical argument. | *Examples:* Apply a mathematical model to illuminate a problem or situation. Conduct a project that specifies a problem, identifies solution paths, solves the problem, and reports results. Design a mathematical model to inform and solve a practical or abstract situation. |

Do you see the deeper structure? It's more comprehensive, which provides a strong gauge of the rigor of an assignment. Notice that although Levels 1 and 2 are important, Levels 3 and 4 are considered rigorous.

4. Students Deserve Empirically Validated Practices

There are many different organizations and researchers who claim effectiveness for their implementation. Some of these do not have empirically validated recommendations. Thus, there is a buyer-beware clause for each individual study you read. Instead, look for groups of studies that synthesize information to show effectiveness. Additionally, search for other studies that verify researchers' or organizations' claims. In Chapters 4 and 5, we'll share samples of empirically validated practices, as well as instructional strategies to support those practices.

5. Data Can Be Used to Drive Instructional Decision-Making

Data-driven decision-making should begin at the teacher level. Foundationally, there are three steps teachers should follow to use data to inform instruction.

Collect Data ⟶ Analyze Data ⟶ Modify Instruction

Teachers should collect data on an ongoing basis, including test scores, formative assessment, and observations. Then, analyze the data looking for strengths and weaknesses, with a particular eye toward any potential skill deficits. Finally, instruction should be modified to address any deficits.

A Systems Analysis Feedback Loop allows us to analyze data and make necessary changes concurrently at the classroom, school level, and district level. Although communicate and collaborate appear to occur at only a certain stage, it is important to have ongoing discussions and problem solving throughout.

Systems Analysis Feedback Loop

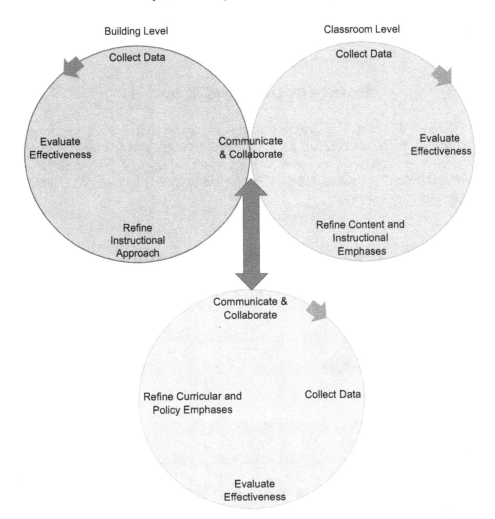

Using the systems analysis feedback loop, teams review their data to evaluate their practices and improve instruction. In addition, district-level teams work with individual school leadership teams and even grade-level or course-level teams to share information. The district with which we work typically has excellent communication between building and grade- and course-level teams, as well as open communication between district leadership and school administration. This feedback loop not only supports such communication but urges districts to set up across-school MTSS teams to discuss strengths and weaknesses. The Pennsylvania Teacher Training Assistance Network (PaTTAN) is well known for bringing schools and districts together to openly share data and approaches so that every participating district is supported (http://pattan.net-website.s3.amazonaws.com/files/materials/publications/docs/RtII-Implement.pdf).

> Which of these five beliefs did you find to be significant? Why?

Intervention: Tiers 2 and 3

There are times that instruction and scaffolding in tier 1 are not enough for students to be successful, and we need to turn to additional support. In the intervention tiers, we advocate for a hybrid approach that addresses the foundational skill and teaches the student to apply that foundational learning to core content.

Intervention vs. Remediation

Carl, a sixth-grader struggling in mathematics, just failed his quiz on the area of trapezoids.

$$A = \frac{(a+b)}{2} h$$

Newbee Middle School is initiating its MTSS approach, but there is a disagreement about the role of the interventionist. Some MTSS leaders want the interventionist to focus on why Carl has difficulty calculating trapezoids (i.e., the distributive property, multiplication, etc.), but some teachers in the building are arguing that Carl's focus, even in intervention, should be on the core lesson: area of a trapezoid. In the first option, the interventionist would teach multiplication skills and Carl would relearn the distributive property. The latter approach, however, requires a focus on practicing what was learned during core instruction with more explanations, description, and use of visuals.

This is an example of the debate surrounding the use of remediation versus intervention. MTSS programs may employ both remediation and intervention approaches. However, there are distinct differences in operationalization and philosophy between the approaches. Remediation is typically thought of as reteaching information that was previously taught but not understood. A concern with remediation is that the reason why the student struggled is not addressed; therefore, that reason will reemerge to cause more difficulties in the future. This is like placing a bandage over a gaping wound, covering only part of the problem.

Intervention, however, focuses on foundational skills that impede the learning of core content. During intervention shouldn't be when and where the students are introduced to an alternate approach. In such cases, the intervention appears disjointed and too unrelated to the core content, making the student think that there are now two math lessons and sets of content rather than one.

Types of Intervention Focus

There are alternatives when it comes to intervention models with MTSS. Although the schedules throughout this chapter provide options to meet common approaches within MTSS, consider alternatives to best meet the academic needs of the students and to utilize the talents within the school.

Boosters

Bryant, Bryant, Gersten, Scammacca, and Chavez (2008) used booster lessons to improve students' mathematics performance. Booster lessons are designed to reinforce instruction taught previously. Oftentimes, booster lessons are tier 2 interventions taught to add to the core curriculum, and they are most effective when they support the core curriculum by teaching students through their deficit areas.

Core Extensions

Core extensions are designed to extend learning time and give students more time to learn the core curriculum. This approach may allow a student more think time regarding the standard and, if taught correctly, it provides the teacher and interventionist the time to enhance the lesson delivery to better meet the needs of the student. For example, the use of visuals and concrete manipulative instruction is highly effective for low-performing students. However, these instructional tools require more time for implementation. A core extension allows for that time.

Core extensions are frequently used in schools but, at least with mathematics, have inconsistent results. Henry, Barrett, and Marder (2016) found only minor differences between the mathematics performance of elementary students in core extensions versus those not in core extensions. However, effects were more marked with middle school students. Still, it may be that double-dosing and core extensions are not the most effective or efficient approach for remediating students with academic concerns. This is likely because the deficit area is not being specifically addressed. In other words, the effectiveness of core extensions has less to do with providing more time and more to do with what is actually happening during that time.

Although core extensions and double-dosing are most often used for intervention purposes, students with academic gifts may benefit from core extensions if they are included in an enrichment program. Henry, Barrett, and Marder (2016) found that "Students who received a double dose for enrichment were the only group whose average previous-year math performance on the North Carolina state test was above that of students who received a single dose" (p. 11). In a gifted extension program, students may acquire foundational skills during core instructional time and then apply or practice generalization during the extension time. In an accelerated gifted program, students will have more time to cover more lessons.

Students in behavioral interventions may also benefit from core extensions. The behavioral intervention is based directly on the interactions that were had or will be had during core instructional time. For example, a student who is receiving behavioral support at the tier 2 level may benefit from a social story review of group work before going into her social studies class, where she is working with a group of students to develop a presentation on Francis Scott Key.

Preteaching

Another option within intervention is to preteach academic content. Many students who receive additional or clarifying instruction on content after it is taught may start to develop a dependency on that support. If students believe that they are less successful in the core classroom than they are during their support class, then they have the tendency to ignore core instruction and simply wait for the support class to explain what they didn't understand, or worse, didn't try to learn.

Preteaching is when the support or intervention class prepares the students for the upcoming core content instruction. When the content is scaffolded in this way, the students experience much of the instruction that they will see in the core and can contribute more readily to the conversation in the core. For example, in a fifth-grade class learning to compute fractions, the preteaching class may have already retaught the differences between numerators and denominators and how computation is performed accordingly. Then, the group would practice appropriate computation skills nearly matching those needed in the upcoming lesson. With this preparation, the students would enter the core instruction having already been exposed to and practiced the content. This may make them more confident with the material and competent with the level of conversation (Lalley & Miller, 2006). Such confidence and competence may eventually increase students' academic learning time and thus their performance.

Although there is some support for preteaching, there are also roadblocks. Much preparation must go into the content and instructional design so that the core content teacher and the interventionist use the same approach. For more information, see http://nycdoeit.airws.org/pdf/Preteaching.pdf.

> Have you used any of these types of intervention focus? Is there one you would like to try?

Organizing Intervention Instruction

During the interventions themselves, intensity should be handled differently at different times based on a student's needs. Considerations should include whether the intervention should only focus on the deficit skill or whether the intervention should dedicate time to tie the deficit skill to the core instruction. For example, a second-grader is learning to recount stories per the standard:

CCSS.ELA-Literacy.RL.2.2

Recount stories, including fables and folktales from diverse cultures, and determine their central message, lesson, or moral.

The second-grader also receives tier 2 intervention with basic decoding. In order to focus on the intervention but address the core, the interventionist would spend a majority of the time focused on decoding but then connect the decoding to the fables used in the core classroom. As such, it is important to help students see the reason why they are in intervention.

Tier 2

During a tier 2 intervention, the interventionist must spend a majority of the time focused on the student's deficit area. However, there are other needs to be met in an intervention. According to Gersten et al. (2008, 2009), the interventionist must provide for motivation and assessment needs in addition to the focused explicit and systematic instruction. Nonstrategic learners often struggle with motivation in school. For logical reasons, few people enjoy doing something they struggle with. In an MTSS program, students are asked to do nearly twice as much. So, in order to keep the student engaged during the intervention, the interventionist must include motivational strategies. A focus on relevance, increased interactions, and even performance self-tracking are excellent ways to increase motivation. Assessment of the intervention's effectiveness is needed to justify the need for the intervention and inform the MTSS team of performance changes and next steps.

Possible Schedule for 30-Minute Tier 2 Intervention

5 minutes: Welcome and introduce the intervention work for the day.
15 minutes: Intervention focus.
5 minutes: Intervention assessment.
5 minutes: Connect intervention to the core content.

Tier 3

During a tier 3 intervention, you should expect to witness increased teacher-to-student interactions, more concrete or physical manipulations for learning, and a steady pace of instruction. Although some intervention programs attempt to replace the core curriculum, we advise that the focus should be on supporting the core curriculum and working at a fast, steady pace designed to address as many deficit skills as possible.

Possible Schedule for a 45-Minute Tier 3 Intervention

5 minutes: Welcome and introduce the intervention work for the day.
30 minutes: Intervention focus.
5 minutes: Intervention assessment.
5 minutes: Connect intervention to the core content.

Intervention Deficit Content

Whether examining interventions or developing your own, it is important to focus on critical content. Intervention needs are considered deficit areas because they are missing from a student's skillset or background. As such, interventions should be specifically based on students' deficit needs. These needs should be evident from assessment data (see Chapter 6).

The following list of common deficit needs is based on reviews of several Institute of Education Sciences (IES) practice guides.

List of Common Deficit Needs

Behavior
    Interactions with peers and adults
    Academic attitude and motivation
    Bullying.

Literacy
    Segments of sounds in speech
    Alphabet awareness connected to phonemes
    Decoding
    Word recognition
    Inferential and narrative language
    Vocabulary knowledge
    Reading comprehension
    Oral reading fluency.
Mathematics
    Number sense
    Computational fluency
    Fractions magnitude
    Rational number computation
    Word problem solving
    Two- and three-dimensional shapes.

For more information on content and instruction from these practice guides, visit the IES websites associated with Epstein, Atkins, Cullinan, Kutash, & Weaver, 2008; Foorman et al., 2016; Frye et al., 2013; Gersten et al., 2008; Gersten et al., 2009; Shanahan et al., 2010; and Woodward et al., 2012.

Which of these areas have you seen in your students? How have you addressed these needs?

Intervention Delivery

Intervention delivery is important. If a school or district is purchasing an intervention, it must first focus on what content must be addressed. Although a school and district must do much internal data collection and analysis to determine the content of interventions, selection of the intervention delivery approach is clear and rather uniform. Overwhelming amounts of research data have proven that tier 2 and 3 interventions should be delivered explicitly and systematically (Gersten et al., 2008; Gersten et al., 2009). Explicit and systematic intervention delivery requires careful, planned preparation, a clear opening, accurate and efficient modeling, guided practice, independent practice, informed decision-making regarding student performance, and a thoughtful approach to maintenance of information. For more information on explicit and systematic instruction, see Chapter 4.

A School-Wide Structure for Tiers 2 and 3

Scheduling is the most important task when initiating an MTSS program. Scheduling core classes is difficult enough without requiring interventions. Between rotating lunch times, recess times (in elementary school), peak hours for student attention, specials (e.g., music, physical education, art), Carnegie Units (middle school and high school), and a multitude of other factors, there is no one way that scheduling works perfectly for each school or district. Adding times for interventions at multiple levels makes it even more complex. The expectation is that tier 2 will require a minimum additional 30 minutes per day per group and tier 3 will require a minimum additional 45 minutes per day per group. Thus, the more groups requiring intervention, the more complex the schedule is to develop and navigate. No matter the outcome for scheduling, problems will likely occur.

As stated by Ted Gennerman, District Director of Assessment and Student Services, and Jennifer Gennerman, Data Specialist, "Scheduling is one of the more challenging aspects of a successful RTI framework considering all of the draws on teacher time" (Gennerman & Gennerman, 2016). MTSS teams must demand the expected number of minutes per intervention to be upheld.

Let's look at sample simplified school schedules.

Grade 3	
Schedule Event	*Times*
Students Arrive	7:45–7:55
Mathematics	7:55–8:55
Mathematics Intervention Groups	8:55–9:25
Recess	9:25–9:45
Core Reading	9:45–11:15
Lunch	11:45–12:15
Literacy Intervention Groups	12:15–12:55
Specials (Art, Music, Computer)	12:55–1:25
Physical Education	1:25–1:55
Science or Social Studies	1:55–2:40
Prepare for Dismissal	2:40–2:50

The organization of this schedule provides a student at least 30 minutes of intervention in mathematics and 40 minutes in literacy. However, there is flexibility in this schedule to allow for up to 60 minutes of tier 3 intervention, the most intense, in either math or literacy.

	Grade 8				
	Monday	*Tuesday*	*Wednesday*	*Thursday*	*Friday*
1st period	8:00–8:50	8:00–8:50	8:00–8:50	8:00–8:50	8:00–8:50
2nd period	8:55–9:45	8:55–9:45	8:55–9:45	8:55–9:45	8:55–9:45
3rd period	9:50–10:40	9:50–10:40	9:50–10:40	9:50–10:40	9:50–10:40
Intervention period	10:45–11:15	10:45–11:15	10:45–11:15	10:45–11:15	10:45–11:15
Lunch	11:15–11:50	11:15–11:50	11:15–11:50	11:15–11:50	11:15–11:50
4th period	11:50–12:40	11:50–12:40	11:50–12:40	11:50–12:40	11:50–12:40
5th period	12:45–1:35	12:45–1:35	12:45–1:35	12:45–1:35	12:45–1:35
6th period	1:40–2:30	1:40–2:30	1:40–2:30	1:40–2:30	1:40–2:30
7th period/ extra intervention period	2:35-3:05	2:35-3:05	2:35-3:05	2:35-3:05	2:35–3:05

Although the elementary schedule provides more flexibility to implement multiple interventions, a traditional secondary schedule is hindered by Carnegie Units. In this schedule, a student has two opportunities through mini-periods to receive 30-minute interventions. In other schedules, however, a student may have to miss a course, such as a special, in order to make room for a full period of interventions.

Other options exist within school schedules, such as flexible scheduling, where days per week are scheduled differently, and block scheduling, where students receive extended time per day in certain courses. When block scheduling is implemented, consider using a daily course around lunch time when interventions may be scheduled. The daily approach allows for the consistency of the intervention and a more flexible time for students to move in and out of the intervention setting.

Conclusion

Within the MTSS program, it's important to focus on prevention first. Ideally, we can provide appropriate support for students within core instruction. In the core classroom, as with all tiers, we want to balance rigorous expectations with scaffolding to ensure success. When students do need additional, more specialized instruction, tiers 2 and 3 provide that opportunity. However, rather than simply focus on remediating deficit skills, intervention is the focus, which allows students to build their skills with an eye toward core instruction.

4

Evidence-Based Instructional Strategies

From core to intervention, it is critical to use rigorous, evidence-based instructional strategies within the MTSS framework. Too often, we simply implement the latest program or jump on the newest bandwagon without considering whether they are effective or rigorous. John Hattie (2008), in his classic meta-analysis of educational studies, found that RTI/MTSS was one of the most effective strategies that impacts student achievement, along with comprehensive interventions for students with learning disabilities.

In this chapter and in Chapter 5, we focus on the specific instructional strategies that are most effective within MTSS. Here, we discuss general recommendations, direct and explicit instruction, and math strategies. Literacy strategies, including those for all curriculum areas, will be shared in Chapter 5. In both chapters, you'll find classroom-based activities that can be used and adapted for all grade levels and subject areas, depending on the strategy. First, let's look at general evidence-based recommendations that can be used in all subjects.

General Recommendations	
Recommendation	*Source*
Teacher clarity.	Hattie (2008, 2012).
Explicit and systematic instruction.	Gersten and colleagues (2009).
Direct instruction.	Hattie (2008, 2012).

(Continued)

(Continued)

Offer on-task classroom discussions.	Hattie (2008, 2012).
Provide formative evaluations.	Hattie (2008, 2012).
Allow for self-questioning.	Hattie (2008, 2012).
Offer frequent, corrective feedback.	Gersten and colleagues (2009), Marzano (2004), Hattie (2008, 2012).
Use non-linguistic representations.	Marzano (2004), Hattie (2008, 2012).

Explicit Instruction

Gersten and colleagues (2009) found that the highest effect size in several of their meta-analyses was in the use of systematic and explicit instruction. Do not confuse systematic and explicit instruction with isolated modeling and little interaction, which is "less rigorous or constrained to basic skill acquisition" (North Carolina MTSS Leadership Team, 2016). Instead, explicit and systematic instruction is complex, involving multiple steps in preparation, presentation, gradually increasing student independence, and assessment. Archer and Hughes (2011) described 16 components that should be considered in tier 1 or core instruction and are imperative to intervention delivery.

16 Components Imperative to Intervention Delivery

1. Focus instruction on critical content.
2. Sequence skills logically.
3. Break complex skills into smaller steps—supported by Hattie, Masters, & Birch's (2015) meta-analysis (ES = 0.87).
4. Design focused lessons.
5. Set the expectation to start the lesson—supported by Marzano, Pickering, and Pollock, (2001).

6. Review prior skills—supported by Marzano (2001).
7. Demonstrate stepwise instructions.
8. Use clear and concise language.
9. Provide examples and non-examples.
10. Provide students guided practice—supported by Marzano (2001).
11. Require frequent responses.
12. Monitor student performance closely.
13. Provide immediate feedback (corrective or affirmative)—supported by Hattie, Masters, & Birch's (2015) meta-analytic work (ES = 0.73).
14. Deliver instruction at a brisk pace.
15. Connect information across lessons and content.
16. Provide abundant time for practice and cumulative review—supported by Marzano (2001).

Although an intensive lesson would include many of these components, if not all of them, it is unlikely to see each of these in a string of lessons. However, at the heart of explicit instruction is a highly interacted dialogue between the teacher and students. This interaction explains the materials, explains the process of thinking and solving problems, and provides feedback for student work. Teachers think aloud as they solve problems, which models for students what they should be thinking.

Explicit and systematic instruction, in a basic sense, may be broken down into four main steps.

Four Steps

Me: Teacher modeling stepwise process while thinking aloud at a brisk pace, presenting both examples and non-examples.

We: High amounts of dialogue between teacher and students.

Two: Paired students engaging in one or two problems, in either a tutorial model or in modeling and checking each other's work.

You: Independent practice for the student.

Throughout this process, the teacher provides immediate and corrective feedback for the student. When lessons focus on the critical content, the use of Me, We, Two, You can be highly effective as an explicit instruction implementation method. Although this may appear straightforward, much preparation must go into the think-aloud involved with modeling and guided practice. The following is an adaptation of Hughes's (2016) example of modeling and guiding practice in mathematics:

½(6x + 4) − 4 = 16	
Modeling (written and spoken)	Guided practice (spoken and written one step behind students at first, then two steps, then three)
"Paper and pencil down; eyes up front as I show you how to solve this problem. I will complete two problems for you and then you will begin to help me."	"Let's solve this problem together."
"First, I see that there is one variable, x, in parentheses on the left side of the equal sign and a constant, 16, on the right side of the equal sign."	"What do the terms of this equation mean?" "What is happening in this equation?"
"Since I am solving for x, I will need to isolate it. So, I add 4 to both sides of the equation. Negative 4 plus 4 is 0 on the left side. On the right, 16 plus 4 is 20. What does the equation read now? ½(3x + 4) = 20."	"What is the goal of your work with this equation?" "What is my first step? Why?"
"Next, I need to calculate the distribution across the parentheses. Since I cannot simplify what is in the parentheses, I will multiply the ½ to both terms. One-half times $6x$ is $3x$, and ½ times 4 is 2. What does the equation read now? 3x + 2 = 20."	"What is our next step? Why?" "What will my new equation be?"
"Since I am still isolating the variable, I will subtract 2 from both sides. 2 minus 2 is 0, and 20 minus 2 is 18. Am I done? No, the x is not isolated yet."	"What is our next step? Why?" "What will my new equation be?"

"I will divide both sides by the coefficient, 3. On the left side, 3 divided by 3 is 1. I have 1x. On the right side, 18 divided by 3 is 6. It appears that 1x is equal to 6."	"What is our next step? Why?" "What will my new equation be?"
"Am I done? No, I must check my work. I erase the x and place 6 in its place. Now, following the order of operations on the left side, I see that 6 times 6 is 36. 36 plus 4 is 40. Since ½ is outside the parenthesis, ½ times 40 is 20. To finish the left side, 20 minus 4 is 16. The equation now reads 16 = 16. Excellent! We did it."	"Am I done calculating?" "How can you check to make sure you solved it correctly?" "Is our answer correct?"

Although explicit and systematic instruction appears intense, an even more intense version of explicit and systematic instruction is direct instruction. Hattie, Masters, and Birch (2015) found moderate effects with direct instruction (ES = 0.60), which is designed to use explicit instruction with increased choral responses, or responses given by students in unison, to help students master small amounts of information at a time through in a thoughtfully sequenced and scaffolded curriculum. Content typically associated with direct instruction is rote memory items requiring less conceptual understanding. Proponents point to its performance-based outcomes effectiveness. Opponents argue that it is too shallow in depth (www.evidencebasedteaching.org.au/direct-instruction-facts-myths/). However, when teaching information requiring memorization and recall, direct instruction is an effective strategy.

Steps for Direct Instruction

1. State the objectives of the lesson, and explain why these objectives are important.
2. Review skills or knowledge necessary to learn the new information.
3. Present the new information in an organized manner.
4. Question students or infuse activities that check for understanding.
5. Provide guided practice.
6. Assess.
7. Provide more opportunities for practice in the form of homework.

Source: RTI Success: Proven Tools and Strategies for Schools and Classrooms by Elizabeth Whitten, Kelli Esteves, and Alice Woodrow.

How have you incorporated direct or explicit instruction in your teaching? What new information did you learn?

Classroom Discussions

There are a variety of activities you can use in your classroom to provide opportunities for students to practice effective speaking and listening skills. Let's look at nine examples.

Nine Examples

Pair-Shares.
Think-Aloud Pair (Triad) Problem Solving.
Conver-Stations.
Discussion Starters.
Jigsaw.
You've Got Mail.
The Brain's Speech Bubble.
Morning Meetings That Spark Discussion.
Paideia or Socratic Seminars.

Pair-Shares

You may already use pair-shares or think-pair-shares in your classroom. In this activity, during your instruction you ask students to reflect on the content, turn to a partner, and share the answer to a question. Then, several students share their answers with the whole group.

There's an easy way to switch this to make it more effective. When students share with the whole group, they share their partner's answer, not their own. This is more rigorous, encourages them to listen better, and requires their partner to do a better job explaining their answer.

Think-Aloud Pair (Triad) Problem Solving

Think-aloud pair (triad) problem solving is an adapted think-pair-share model from Lochhead and Whimbey (1987).

Think-Aloud Pair (Triad) Problem Solving

Divide students into groups of three.

Give each group a problem to solve, a text (or image) to interpret, or a case history to discuss.

Ask students to designate an explainer, a questioner, and a recorder.

The explainer explains how to solve the problem, interpret the text (or image), or analyze the case.

The questioner asks questions when the explanation is not clear or is incomplete. The questioner can also ask questions to give hints that might generate new or different explanations.

The recorder records the explanation via writing notes and/or drawing diagrams.

After 10 minutes, ask each explainer to present the explanation, using the recorder's notes. As a follow-up, you might discuss what types of questions were most helpful in refining the explanation and why.

Conver-Stations

Sarah Brown Wessling, a former National Teacher of the Year, describes Conver-Stations, which is an alternate way to inspire discussion. Students are placed into a few groups of four to six students each and given a discussion question to talk about. After a few moments (you'll need to decide the appropriate amount of time), one or two students from each group will rotate to a different group. Once in their new group, they discuss a different but related question, and they also share some of the key points from their last group's conversation. For the next rotation, students who have not yet rotated move, resulting in groups that are continually evolving.

Discussion Starters

Discussion starters are sentence frames or starters that help students express ideas and interact with one another about learning. These can be as simple as *who, what, when, where, why, how,* and *which,* or they can be more structured.

Jigsaw

Jigsaw is a form of cooperative learning that structures opportunities for group discussion. In the jigsaw method of teaching, students are placed in small groups, assigned a topic, move with other students assigned the same topic, research the information, then return to their original group as an expert to teach the material, and this is a way of increasing the rigor of a teacher's lessons. Students are required to work at high levels to accomplish the task.

Jigsaw in 10 Easy Steps

1. Divide students into four- or five-person jigsaw groups. The groups should be diverse in terms of gender, ethnicity, race, and ability.
2. Appoint one student from each group as the leader. Initially, this person should be the most mature student in the group.
3. Divide the day's lesson into five or six segments. For example, if you want history students to learn about Eleanor Roosevelt, you might divide a short biography of her into stand-alone segments on her childhood, her family life with Franklin and their children, her life after Franklin contracted polio, her work in the White House as first lady, and her life and work after Franklin's death.
4. Assign each student to learn one segment, making sure students have direct access only to their own segment.
5. Give students time to read over their segment at least twice and become familiar with it. There is no need for them to memorize it.
6. Form temporary "expert groups" by having one student from each jigsaw group join other students assigned to the same segment. Give students in these expert groups time to discuss the main points of their segment and to rehearse the presentations they will make to their jigsaw group.
7. Bring the students back into their jigsaw groups.
8. Ask each student to present his or her segment to the group. Encourage others in the group to ask questions for clarification.
9. Float from group to group, observing the process. If any group is having trouble (e.g., a member is dominating or disruptive), make an appropriate intervention. Eventually, it's best for the group leader to handle this task. Leaders can be trained by whispering an instruction on how to intervene until the leader gets the hang of it.
10. At the end of the session, give a quiz on the material so that students quickly come to realize that these sessions are not just fun and games but really count.

You've Got Mail

In a resource on ways to check for understanding, Edutopia (www.edutopia.org/resource/checking-understanding-download) recommends using You've Got Mail. As the author describes it,

> Each student writes a question about a topic on the front of an envelope; the answer is included inside. Questions are then "mailed" around the room. Each learner writes his or her answer on a slip of scratch paper and confirms its correctness by reading the "official answer" before she places his or her own response in the envelope. After several series of mailings and a class discussion about the subject, the envelopes are deposited in the teacher's letterbox.

The Brain's Speech Bubble

Carolyn Chapman and Rita King, in their book *Differentiated Assessment Strategies; One Tool Doesn't Fit All*, recommend an activity called The Brain's Speech Bubble.

The Brain's Speech Bubble

1. Make a large speech bubble.
2. Select a student to act as the speaker, or have the teacher explain his or her inside thinking while solving a problem.
3. Each time the person tells his or her thinking for a step, the bubble is held directly above the speaker's head. The speaker stands beneath the speech bubble as he or she verbalizes the brain's thinking for the class.
4. The speaker moves away from the speech bubble when not voicing his or her inside thinking to the class.

Before

Is my mind focused on the task?
Do I have what I need to get started?
How do I get started?
How can I organize my thoughts?

It's an interesting way for students to demonstrate their thinking, as well as interact with the class.

Morning Meetings That Spark Discussion

Jenny Johansson creates listening opportunities for her special education students through inquiry-based morning meetings. For the first 5–20 minutes of class, she focuses on independent inquiry. Students generate questions on a variety of subjects and read books and articles about their topics.

> Then we get together in a circle on the floor for CPR [Circle of Power and Respect] for the actual meeting. During the independent inquiry time, they could sign up to actively participate in the meeting. The routine of the meeting includes a greeting, poetry, book recommendation, and inquiry sharing. During the greeting, they hear their name said in a positive light by their peers each day. During inquiry sharing students get to share with us what they are currently becoming an expert on. Student interests are really developed during this time.

During the discussions, she enhances the student's listening through involvement and ownership. As she noted, "They are so motivated by their own voices being heard."

Paideia or Socratic Seminar

Another type of discussion is a Paideia or Socratic seminar, which shifts the role of the teacher to that of a facilitator and emphasizes each student's contribution to the discussion. As Marcia Alexander, a high school teacher, explains,

> Paideia seminar has been the most successful teaching tool that I have used because it gives students the opportunity to

demonstrate their knowledge and concerns about an issue that they can relate to.

For example, I may have students read an excerpt written by Sojourner Truth, a woman and an African American former slave, abolitionist, and speaker of women's rights. The discussion topic is discrimination and I create open-ended questions, such as "Does being illiterate make a person less intelligent?"

In her role as a facilitator, Marcia ensures that every student speaks at least once before she poses another open-ended question. The nature of the discussion requires that students actively listen to each other in order to respond appropriately.

Cooperative Learning Rubric

	You're a Team Player!	*You're Working on It . . .*	*You're Flying Solo*
G **Group** **Dedication**	The student is totally dedicated to his or her group, offering all of his or her attention by actively listening to peers and responding to others.	The student is partially dedicated to his or her group but sometimes becomes distracted by students or issues outside the group.	The student spends most of his or her time focusing on things outside of the group; he or she is not available for discussion or group work.
R **Responsibility**	The student shares responsibility equally with other group members and accepts his or her role in the group.	The student takes on responsibility but does not completely fulfill his or her obligations.	The student either tries to take over the group and does not share responsibilities or takes no part at all in the group work assigned.

(Continued)

(Continued)

O **Open Communication**	The student gives polite and constructive criticism to group members when necessary, welcomes feedback from peers, resolves conflict peacefully, and asks questions when a group goal is unclear.	The student gives criticism, though often in a blunt manner; reluctantly accepts criticism from peers; and may not resolve conflict peacefully all of the time.	The student is quick to point out the faults of other group members, yet is unwilling to take any criticism in return; often, the student argues with peers rather than calmly coming to a consensus.
U **Utilization of Work Time**	The student is always on task, working with group members to achieve goals, objectives, and deadlines.	The student is on task most of the time but occasionally takes time off from working with the group.	The student does not pay attention to the task at hand and frustrates other group members because of his or her inability to complete work in a timely fashion.
P **Participation**	The student is observed sharing ideas, reporting research findings to the group, taking notes from other members, and offering assistance to his or her peers as needed.	The student sometimes shares ideas or reports findings openly but rarely takes notes from other group members.	The student does not openly share ideas or findings with the group, nor does he or she take notes on peers' findings.

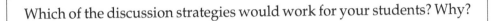

Which of the discussion strategies would work for your students? Why?

Formative Evaluations

Characteristics of Formative Assessment

If we accept that formative assessment is a critical part of our classrooms, then we need to determine what effective formative assessment is. In her book *Rigor and Assessment in the Classroom*, Barbara shared nine characteristics of effective formative assessment.

Effective FORMATIVE Assessment

Focus is on improving teaching and learning.
Ownership of assessment shared by teacher and students.
Requires feedback to move learning forward.
Metacognition and self-assessment encouraged.
Activates students to be peer assessors.
Takes place during instruction.
Identifies where a student is and helps him or her move forward.
Variety of frequent assessments.
Examples of goals and grading criteria provided.

Focus Is on Improving Teaching and Learning

First, with effective formative assessment, the focus is on improving teaching and learning. It may seem self-evident that improving learning is a purpose of formative assessment, but it can also improve your teaching. We can learn from formative assessment where our instruction has been effective and where we need to improve.

Ownership of Assessment Shared by Teacher and Students

Because formative assessment affects both students and teachers, the ownership is shared. This is a shift from traditional assessment approaches that are teacher-focused. By including students in the process, students are more motivated, more engaged, and more apt to learn.

Requires Feedback to Move Learning Forward

A critical aspect of formative assessment is feedback. In fact, it is so important that we've devoted an entire chapter to it: Chapter 9. But for the moment, let's just note that without giving feedback to students, there is no way for them to improve.

Metacognition and Self-Assessment Encouraged

As a part of student ownership, metacognition and self-assessment are encouraged. Learning how to think about their own thinking is a skill students can learn, and it is necessary for improved learning. If they can't assess themselves, students are always dependent on the teacher.

Activates Students to Be Peer Assessors

In addition to self-assessment, we should teach students to assess each other. Formative assessment works best in a collaborative environment, not only where the teacher collaborates with students but also where the students collaborate with each other. Providing opportunities for peer assessment, preceded by instruction on how to work together for assessment, is critical.

Takes Place During Instruction

Formative assessment also takes place during instruction, not afterward. If assessment is going to inform teachers and students and transform teaching, as James Popham says, it must occur during instruction. It is woven into the teaching and learning process and is naturally integrated, as opposed to being added on.

Identifies Where a Student Is and Helps Him or Her Move Forward

Another characteristic of formative assessment is that it identifies where students are and helps them move forward. As we've already mentioned, the most effective formative assessment informs both teachers and students. The focus should be on helping students learn, and this happens when you start where students are and move them to new levels of learning.

Variety of Frequent Assessments

Next, formative assessment uses a variety of assessments, and they are used frequently. If we want to work with students to continually improve learning, the assessments need to occur on a regular basis. Additionally, instead of choosing to only use one type of assessment, such as an exit slip, effective teachers use a wide range of assessments to best understand students' strengths and weaknesses.

Examples of Goals and Grading Criteria Provided

Finally, it's important to provide clear goals for students so they understand what they are to learn. Without this understanding, they are not able to self-assess. You also need to provide examples of grading criteria, including rubrics, so that students gain a clear picture of expectations. Clarity in both goals and grading criteria is essential for students to share ownership of learning.

Samples of Formative Assessment

There are a wide range of formative assessment strategies. Some of the common ones are listed below.

Formative Assessment Strategies

Checklists.
Running records.
Observations.
Questions.
Classroom discussions.
Exit slips.
Graphic organizers.
Learning logs.
Individual whiteboards.
Technology options (e.g., clickers).

Former teacher Kendra Alston focuses on comprehension elements through the use of Five Golden Lines. You can use any elements that match your lesson, just be sure that there are enough examples for the number. For example, because there is usually only one theme for a story, that always needs to go with the number 1. Then, put the points on a PowerPoint presentation or on posters and count down with your students, giving them time to write the answers before you move on. It's an excellent activity to use after reading a story, or it can be used as a graphic organizer to help students plan a story of their own.

Five Golden Lines

5. Major plot points such as exposition, rising action, climax, falling action, resolution.
4. Characters.
3. Descriptive words about the setting.
2. Examples of imagery from the story.
1. Theme of the story.

Connie Forrester adapted the elements for her primary-age students as a countdown to help her students "blast off" for comprehension.

Blast Off

3. Connections ("This reminds me of . . .").
2. Visualizations ("This makes me see . . .").
1. Idea ("This makes me think . . .").

Four Corners

Four Corners was originally designed to be used with multiple-choice questions to allow students to physically demonstrate their responses. Students who believed the answer was A would go to the back right corner, B to the back left corner, and so on. Once they were in groups, students discussed the responses. After assessing students' responses, the teacher leads a whole-group discussion; students are given the option to move to another corner as long as they can justify their change, which increases the rigor.

Another alternative a teacher recently shared with us adapts Four Corners so that students demonstrate how well they understand the content.

Corner 1: "Stop!"—I am totally confused.

Corner 2: "Slow Down"—I understand some of it but couldn't pass a test today.

Corner 3: "Keep Moving"—I'm getting it and I hope we won't have too much homework about it.

Corner 4: "Let Me Help"—I understand it and could teach it to my friends.

Once students go to their corners, they have two minutes to generate questions with the other students in that corner about what they are learning. The questions are then posed to the class for clarification and discussion. The questions generally reflect the level of understanding from each corner, and the teacher can quickly address gaps and incorrect learning.

Agree/Disagree

Agree/Disagree can be done physically with students moving to either side of a line, or it can be done in writing by individuals or groups of students.

At the Start of Class			At the End of Class	
Agree	Disagree	Information	Agree	Disagree

This particular strategy allows you to see the growth of learning for each student.

Electronic Exit Tickets

You may already use exit slips or exit tickets, which are simple response forms for students to complete at the end of class. These can be as simple as "What did you learn?" or more complex ones with multiple questions. However, with today's technology, there are a variety of ways to collect this information from your students.

Apps and Resources for
Electronic Exit Tickets

Google Forms.
Plickers.
Twitter.
Socrative.
Geddit.
Poll Everywhere.
ExitTicket.
VoiceThread.
Lino.
Padlet.

CROWN Exit Slips

With CROWN exit slips, a more formal form of an exit slip, students respond to a variety of items to show they understand the content.

CROWN

Communicate what you learned.
React to what you learned.
One-sentence summary.
Way(s) to use what you learned.
Note how well you did today.

Self-Questioning

Self-questioning is when students ask and answer questions while reading. This is what good readers do naturally, thus "improving their active processing of text and their comprehension" (National Reading Panel, 2000, p. 51).

Good Readers' Self-Questioning Strategies

Before Reading

Good readers . . .

1. consider what they already know about the topic.
2. use text features (e.g., headings and illustrations) to get a sense of what they will read.

During Reading

Good readers . . .

1. monitor their reading.
2. use "fix-up" strategies to repair meaning when comprehension problems occur.
3. use context clues to help them figure out the meanings of unknown vocabulary and concepts.
4. identify the main idea.
5. use their knowledge of text structure to help them understand what they are reading.

After Reading

Good readers . . .

1. mentally summarize what they have read.
2. reflect on content.
3. draw inferences to help them make connections to themselves, to other texts, and to the world around them.

Self-Questioning With Prompts

We've found that in many cases, students who are struggling need additional support in the form of prompts or actual questions. Prompts are sentence starters that provide a jumping-off point for students; the full question gives additional help. Although self-questioning is most often discussed for the reading classroom, we find it to be a helpful strategy as students are problem solving in math.

Questions and Question Prompts	
Reading	*Math*
How would you use . . . to . . .? What would happen if . . .? What are the strengths and weaknesses of . . .? Explain why . . . . Why is . . . important? What is the best . . . and why? How does . . . affect . . .? How did the writer help you understand . . .? How did the writer make this book interesting? Look at the way the writer began the book. What did the writer do to get you interested in the topic? What side do you think the writer is on? Why? What is the significance of . . .? How does . . . change? What does . . . learn? How do you think . . . felt when (or about) . . .? Why do you think . . .? Can you give an example from the book? What is the evidence for . . .?	What do you think will be the answer? Is there another way to solve it? Does that make sense? Why did you do . . .? What did you notice? What might . . .? What if you started with . . . instead of . . .? What if you could only use . . .? How is this problem related to other problems you have done? Can you solve a related problem? Can you simplify the problem and then solve it? Can you find connections between this problem and other problems? Can you explain the solution to someone else? Can they explain your solution to you? Can they explain your solution to someone else? Can you explain your solution without words?

(Continued)

(Continued)

Excerpted from https://ctkis. buncombeschools.org/common/ pages/UserFile.aspx?fileId= 3512105 *and* www.wa.gov/esd/ training/toolbox/tg_selfquestioning. htm

Can you explain your solution using only words (no symbols or drawings)?

Are there any technological tools that might make the problem easier to visualize or manipulate?

How can you justify or explain your solution?

If your answer is not unique, how many different answers are there?

How do you know your answer is reasonable?

Can you reflect on your problem-solving process?

How could you change this problem?

Can you think of related problems?

What is interesting about this problem?

How could you generalize this problem?

Excerpted from David Wees https://davidwees.com/content/ questions-ask-while-problem- solving/ *and* www.nd.gov/dpi/ uploads/1382/QuestionStems Promote8MathematicalPractices.pdf

How have you used formative assessment in your classroom so far? Of the recommendations above, which would help your students the most?

Feedback

What does effective feedback look like? It's important to consider because feedback can have a negative effect on students. For example, if the only feedback is whether a question is right or wrong, no additional learning occurs. How can we expect students in all tiers to work at a rigorous level it we don't provide the best possible feedback? Barbara explained the characteristics of effective feedback in *Rigor and Assessment in the Classroom*.

Related to Goals

First, effective feedback is related to goals, objectives, and standards. This sounds basic, but too often we focus our feedback on other, possibly important, items. Barbara observed a teacher whose students completed an analysis of a science experiment, a rigorous task. The goal was clear in terms of analysis and was focused on what the students learned from the experiment, as well as other possible outcomes based on differing variables. When providing written feedback, the first-year teacher wrote most of her comments about the group work and the role each student played. Although this was important, it was not part of the assignment and did not relate to the stated objective. It distracted students from the task at hand.

Timely

Effective feedback is also timely. It is given after initial instruction so that students have an opportunity to be successful. It is also provided soon after students have completed their work. If you wait too long, students tend to forget what they have done, and the feedback is meaningless.

```
┌─────────────────────────────────────────────┐
│        Tips for Providing Efficient Feedback  │
│                                               │
│   Check for completion, with some comments.    │
│   Keep a list of common feedback statements    │
│   as a reference.                              │
│   Use rubrics.                                 │
│   Use peer feedback.                           │
└─────────────────────────────────────────────┘
```

Frequent

Next, feedback should be frequent. The question is, how frequent? Unfortunately, there simply isn't a formula. Sometimes, you will give individual students feedback every day, or even multiple times a day in an elementary classroom. Other times, if you are giving feedback on 150 assignments, it may be once a week. We think the most effective guideline is that feedback should be a regular part of your classroom, and it should be considered in a broad sense. For example, there is verbal feedback as you monitor the class, peer feedback when students are working with a partner or with a small group, self-reflective feedback when students are assessing themselves, and more formal written feedback. Because you are increasing the rigor of your classroom, you want to be sure to incorporate ample feedback so students can understand where they stand.

Specific, Clear, and Accurate

Feedback should also be specific, clear, and accurate. Specificity and clarity are critical; without it, students do not have a clear picture as to what they can and cannot do. For example, it isn't helpful to simply tell a student, "You did a good job with your writing. Keep it up." The student doesn't understand what he or she did to make the writing "good," so he or she doesn't know what to do next time.

Formative

Effective feedback is typically formative, rather than summative. Feedback should help students know how to improve for the future. If feedback is used in a summative manner, it's often too late for students to improve.

Progress-Oriented

As a formative assessment, feedback should focus on progress. Again, feedback should help students move forward. When Barbara was a teacher, sometimes she told students what they did wrong, but she didn't help them understand how to make progress, which leads to our next characteristic.

Focuses on Next Steps

To help students make progress, you'll need to show them the next step they should take. A teacher in one of Barbara's workshops said, "Once I tell them what they didn't do right, they should know what to do next." Barbara's response? If students knew what to do, they would do it. If their work needs improvement, they need your help, and just telling them to improve isn't enough.

Provides Explanations

Feedback that is effective expands on comments to provide an explanation. Let's say you have a student working on a math problem in which he or she answered with a positive number rather than a negative number. You might tell this student, first, "Review the steps in the problem." A deeper explanation would include guiding him or her to remember the rules for adding and subtracting positive and negative integers and asking him or her to explain the steps he or she followed for adding or subtracting to answer the question.

Emphasizes Learning, Not Personality

Effective feedback also emphasizes the student's learning. When students hear feedback that is personal (as opposed to personalized), they don't know what to do with it. If a teacher tells you that you are so smart, what does that tell you about your learning?

Learning-Focused Feedback	*Personality-Focused Feedback*
When you did this, it added to the explanation.	Fantastic!
You did these particular things well.	You did well today.
I noticed that you did this. Why did you do that? How might you do it differently?	You are so smart.

How will these characteristics of effective feedback help you improve your feedback?

Non-Linguistic Representations

Non-linguistic representations, typically referred to as graphic organizers, can be very effective for your students. They present information visually and help students organize their thoughts.

Pizza Wheel

We also like to use a "pizza wheel" to review material that students are assigned to read before class. Rather than simply listing information, using the wheel allows students to visually organize their thinking. Each student writes a fact that he or she learned on one of the pizza slices.

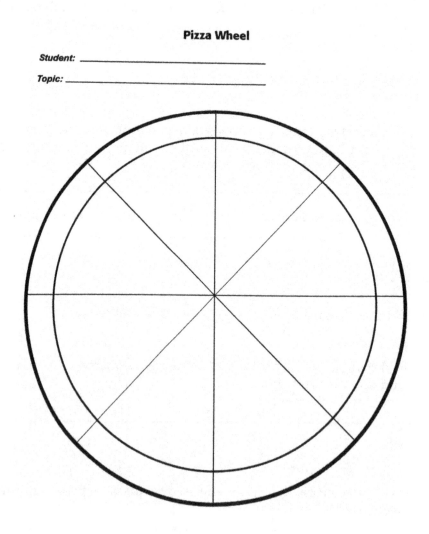

Pizza Wheel

Student: _____

Topic: _____

Then, working in small groups, students pass their papers to the next group member, who also writes a fact. This continues around the circle until each pizza is full. Students can discuss the material using the pizza wheels as a prompt.

Although you can measure your students' understanding in an oral discussion, asking each student to write his or her response ensures that all students are involved in the lesson and provides an opportunity for every student to respond. The rigor is increased as each student is required to participate.

Fishbone

One non-linguistic representation that we find particularly useful is the fishbone graphic organizer. The fishbone is used to explore aspects of a complex topic. It is particularly helpful if a student has a single, complicated topic and then needs to detail more information on ideas, examples, or attributes. The fishbone helps students focus, monitor their comprehension, and organize information as they complete the organizer. It also helps them see gaps where they need to find more information.

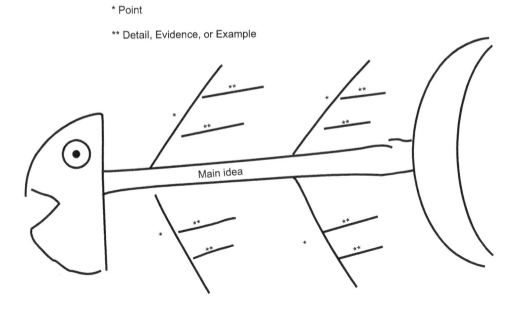

* Point

** Detail, Evidence, or Example

Main idea

CUBES

A commonly used process for solving math problems is CUBES. Warning: the use of keywords in word problems has not had consistent success. However, if keywords are emphasized, then a metacognitive strategy to guide the use of keywords is warranted. Following is a sample chart with the steps and visuals that can help students follow the steps.

C	(1) (6) (2) (7) (3) (8) (4) (9) (5) (0)	Circle the number.
U	?	Underline the question.
B	[ ]	Box the keywords.
E	(X)	Eliminate what you don't need.
S	(magnifying glass)	Solve by showing your work.

The non-linguistic representation students would complete is below. Once you teach students the system, they can complete this representation as an anchor chart in groups or individually on a handout.

(1) (6) (2) (7) (3) (8) (4) (9) (5) (0)	Problem
?	Solution

In *Rigor Is Not a Four-Letter Word*, Barbara shared a graphic organizer for solving word problems developed by a school with a large percentage of high-needs students. It helps students break down the problem-solving process and focus on the math tasks.

Graphic Organizer for Math Word Problems

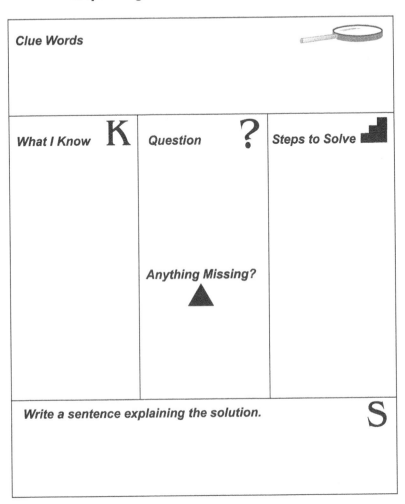

Conclusion

When it comes to interventions and working with students who have a history of academic difficulties, there is no such thing as "I've tried everything!" There are simply too many instructional options to have tried everything. Instead, when working with students with academic difficulties, start with proven instructional methods, such as explicit and systematic instruction and others listed in this chapter. Use these strategies across several weeks with fidelity in order to give the student another chance at a successful future.

Models of Proficient Problem Solving

Teach How to Solve a Problem

The first step for students to become proficient at problem solving is to teach them how to do so. Teach strategies for solving problems, model their uses, and provide plenty of opportunity to practice.

Strategies for Solving a Problem

Estimate.
Guess and check.
Use logical reasoning.
Draw a picture.
Create a chart or table.
Make a list.
Look for a pattern.
Break it into parts.
Set up an equation.
Work backward.
Act it out.
Solve a simpler problem.

Provide Practice With Problem Solving

In addition to teaching students learning problem-solving strategies, provide opportunities for them to work at rigorous levels. Let's take a look at a sample kindergarten graphing lesson from Henry County, Georgia. Students were given a Ziploc bag with small candy bunnies and were asked to sort them by color. Then, they used a simple graph to show how many bunnies of each color they had. Typically, we have students complete the graph. However, to increase the rigor, the teachers asked questions at the end in which they not only compared items, but they had to evaluate any misconceptions they had.

For example, the teacher would choose one student's (or group's) graph and show it to the group. Then, he or she would describe something about the graph, providing an incorrect answer. For example, the teacher might say, "in this graph, there are more blue bunnies than red bunnies." "Am I correct or not? How do you know?" Here are two things I know <insert two statements>. "Which one is wrong? Why?" "Now, fix it." By identifying and correcting misconceptions, students demonstrated a higher level of thinking.

Sample Middle School Mathematics Performance Task

Next, let's look at a middle school sample in which students must design their own sudoku puzzles. Imagine the problem solving that must occur in this rigorous activity.

Mathemagic: Exploring Sudoku and Other Magic Squares

Grade Level: 6th and up

The **goals** of this project are

1. To experiment with magic square design
2. To find new uses for magic squares

Research Questions

1. What is the history of magic squares?
2. What are their applications, other than sudoku puzzles?

A magic square is a mathematical construct in which symbols (usually numbers) are arranged in a square so that the numbers in all rows, columns, and diagonals add up to the same amount. No symbol can appear more than once in any row, column, or diagonal. Magic squares have been known to mankind for thousands of years and are sometimes associated with ceremonial magic. In contemporary culture, they most commonly appear in those form of those ever-so-popular puzzles known as sudoku. In this project, we explore other uses for magic squares.

Materials

1. Computer with internet access
2. Color printer

3. Digital camera
4. Typical office/hobby/hardware/craft supplies (paper, poster board, glue, wood, etc.)

All materials can be found in your home, at local stores, or on eBay.

Experimental Procedure

Read overview of relevant topics. Search and print out interesting images that seem appropriate to this project. Address all of the above research questions.

Take your own photographs throughout the course of the experiment.

Create your own sudoku puzzle variations, using colors, shapes, or whatever you like. Fill a 3×3 or 4×4 grid with letters. Try to create a magic square poem or anagram. Design your own magic square art forms.

Think of a new way to use magic squares (optional).

Carefully record your experiences.

Analyze your data.

Interpret your findings in a detailed report.

Include interesting photos, diagrams, and art in your science fair display.

Source: www.education.com/science-fair/article/mathematics-magic-squares/

Finally, let's look at a high school math problem. Once again, consider how much students are asked to use higher levels of thinking as they solve the problem.

Sample High School Mathematics Performance Task

Golf Balls in Water

Part A: Students analyze data from an experiment involving the effect on the water level of adding golf balls to a glass of water in which they:

- Explore approximately linear relationships by identifying the average rate of change.
- Use a symbolic representation to model the relationship.

Part B: Students suggest modifications to the experiment to increase the rate of change.

Part C: Students interpret linear functions using both parameters by examining how results change when a glass with a smaller radius is used by:

◆ Explaining how the *y*-intercepts of two graphs will be different
◆ Explaining how the rate of change differs between two experiments
◆ Using a table, equation, or other representation to justify how many golf balls should be used

Source: Herman, J. L., & Linn, R. L. (2013). *On the road to assessing deeper learning: The status of Smarter Balanced and PARCC assessment consortia* (C RESST Report No. 823). Los Angeles: University of California, National Center for Research on Evaluation, Standards, and Student Testing, as found in Darling-Hammond and Adamson (2014), *Next Generation Assessment: Moving Beyond the Bubble Test to Support 21st Century Learning.*

> What is an example of a task, assignment, or assessment that reflects rigorous problem solving?

Verbalize Thought Processes

Verbalizing your thinking is an important part of mathematics instruction. The purpose is to model what strategic learners do in order to solve problems.

Example of a Think-Aloud

Word Problem

Alex was going to buy a new video game at GameStop. The original price of the game was $79, and it's currently on sale for 10% off. Determine the cost of the game.

Sample Think-Aloud

I need to start by figuring out what this problem is asking. When I reread the problem, I notice it's asking me to determine the cost of the game [underline in text]. *So that's important—I have to find the cost of the game at GameStop. Now I'll go back to the problem and see what information I can use to figure this out. It tells me the game cost $79* [circle in word problem] *and that it's on sale—10% off* [circle in text].

Now that I have this information, I need to figure out what to do with it. I know from my shopping experiences that when something is discounted, I need to figure out how much the discount is in dollars and then subtract that from the original price. So I'm ready to start doing the math [all the math will be recorded throughout the think-aloud].

The original price is $79. In order to figure out how much the discount is, I need to multiply the price by the 10% discount. To do that, I need to change 10% to a decimal, 0.1. So I'll take 79 × 0.1 and that gives me 7.9 or $7.90. So that's the discount. Now I need to calculate what the cost of the game would be. I'll take the original price, $79, and subtract the discount, $7.90, to find the sale price [79 − 7.90 = 71.1], which would be $71.10.

Now I'll look back at the word problem to be sure I've solved it. It asks me to determine the cost of the game. And I've done that—the game would cost $71.10.

Source: Content Area Literacy in the Mathematics Classroom,
Abbigail Armstrong, Kavin Ming, and Shawna Helf.

Guided Practice

Guided practice, which we mentioned in the section on direct and explicit instruction, is another important facet of instruction. Think of the model as helping a child learn to ride a bike. First you put the child on a bike with training wheels, then you take the training wheels off but hold on to the seat, then you let go so they can ride it on their own. In teaching, we show students what to do (I do it), then we do the learning with students (we do it), then they do it on their own (you do it). Guided practice is the "we do it" part. Let's take a look at a model.

Let's do one together.
Word problem:
Joseph receives an 18% off coupon for the movie. His movie ticket originally costs $8.50. What is the discounted price of the ticket?
What is the problem asking for? [Wait for answers.] Yes, it's asking for the price of the ticket after we deduct the discount from the coupon.
What information do I need to solve this problem? [Have students list the answers with their neighbors.]
Good. I need the original price and the discount.
How do I compute the discount? [wait]
Yes, I multiply the decimal of the percent, 0.18, times the original price, $8.50.
What do I get? [wait]

> *Good, $1.53. How did you get that?* [Student explains their process and reasoning.]
> > *What does $1.53 represent?* [wait]
> > *Now what?* [Have students work in pairs.]
> > *Yes, I subtract the discount from the original price.*
> > *What do you get?* [wait]
> > *Good, $8.53 − $1.53 = $6.97.*
> > *$6.97 is the discounted price.*

Perform a few guided practices with the class, fading out one or two questions each time. Your last guided practice should be nearly student independent.

Frequent, Cumulative Review

Frequent, cumulative review is also important. Before the end of the lesson, have students complete enough practice problems that you are comfortable they understand the materials and can successfully complete problems independently. Assess the last problem so that you have data to confirm your assertion.

Every week or two, provide an opportunity for students to go back over older work. Give them work from up to six weeks ago, checking that they remember how to solve those problems. Such occasional and planned cumulative review reminds students of processes and practices that are needed across a curriculum. This is particularly needed for students with memory deficits.

Conclusion

Whether we are looking at general strategies across the curriculum or math strategies in particular, it's important to emphasize those that are shown to be effective. It's easy to find strategies, particularly on the internet, that sound or look good but may not be research-based. Let's keep our focus on what we know works.

5

Evidence-Based Practices in Literacy

Now that we have looked at general strategies as well as math ones, let's turn our attention to literacy. One specific challenge with literacy is that it is such a general area, it's hard to home in on specific aspects that can make a difference with students. In this chapter, we look at rigorous, research-based strategies for overall literacy, reading, and writing. You'll note that as we talk about literacy, we focus on literacy across the curriculum, including math.

Literacy Strategies

Writing Recommendations	
Recommendation	*Source*
Have students write about what they read.	Graham and Hebert (2010).
Write summaries and take notes.	Marzano (2004).
Teach students writing skills and processes, especially spelling and sentence construction.	Graham and Hebert (2010).
Increase how much students write.	Graham and Hebert (2010).

Write About Reading

Writing about something you have read is almost an everyday occurrence in classrooms. Students do this by simply answering questions in written form, by summarizing information, or by taking notes.

The Henry County Public Schools outside Atlanta, Georgia, have found the RACE strategy to be extremely effective. Using the RACE strategy, students are asked a question about what they have read, and then they follow the RACE steps.

RESTATE the question.
Reread and restate the question in your topic sentence.

ANSWER the question that is being asked.
Use your answer to write your topic sentence.

CITE evidence from the text.
Use examples and evidence from the text to support your answer.

EXPLAIN your answer.
Explain how the evidence from the text supports your answer.

In Chapter 3, we discussed using Webb's Depth of Knowledge as a benchmark of rigor. DOK Levels 3 and 4 are considered rigorous. The RACE strategy steps are at various levels of DOK. As Melissa Thomas, Assessment and Data Response Facilitator for Henry County Schools, explains,

> The *R* is restate the question, which is Level 1. *A*, answer the question, is either a 1 or a 2, depending on the question. *C*, cite evidence from the text, is still a 2 because students do not go beyond the text. *E*, explain your answer, is where you incorporate rigor. As long as students do not just restate the evidence and bring in their own experiences and examples, *E* is a Level 3. In *E*, students should be making text-to-text connections, text-to-self connections, and text-to-world connections.

The Center Grove Community School Corporation, a public school system in Indiana, provides its teachers with a list of 100 possible question starters and questions for students to use when they respond to their reading (www.centergrove.k12.in.us/cms/lib4/IN01000850/Centricity/Domain/24/100_Reader_Response_PROMPTS.docx). We've excerpted 18 for you that apply across a variety of subject areas.

Questions/Starters to Respond to Reading

1. I wonder what this means . . .
2. I really don't understand the part when . . .
3. I really like/dislike this idea because . . .
4. I think the relationship between _____ and _____ is interesting because . . .
5. This section makes me think about _____ because . . .
6. I'm not sure about . . .
7. When I don't know a word, I . . .
8. What connections are there between the book and your life? Explain.
9. What is the most important sentence/paragraph/passage in this book? The most important event or feeling? Explain.
10. What makes you wonder in this book? What confuses you?
11. Has the book helped you in any way? Explain.
12. What do you know now that you didn't know before?
13. If you were making this book into a movie, what part(s) would you cut out or change? Why?
14. Write a feasible solution for a problem.
15. Give three reasons why this should be taught to the whole class.
16. Make a timeline of the major events (minimum five events) in this story. You must illustrate each event and label each event with a caption or description.
17. List 10 interesting/"expensive" words from your book and . . . (choose only one).
    a. tell why each word is interesting.
    b. write a definition for each word.
    c. use each in a sentence of your own.

Note that "book" may also mean an article or any type of text.

Summarize and Take Notes

Specific ways to respond to reading with writing are summarizing and taking notes.

Summarizing

We often take summarization for granted. Simply write the key points of the discussion or text, and you are done. But summarization is actually more rigorous. In order to effectively summarize information, you must mentally sift through all the given information, prioritize what is and is not important, and then determine the most important information. Let's look at several creative ways for students to summarize information.

Creative Summarization Strategies

Acrostics: Give students a vocabulary word related to the lesson. Ask them to write a word or a phrase starting with each letter of the word.

Concept Posters: Write keywords or key concepts from the text/lesson on posters around the room. Ask students to rotate around the room, writing their key points on the posters.

$2 Summaries: Ask students to write a summary that totals $2.00. Each word is worth 10 cents.

Tweet: Write a 140-character tweet summarizing the material.

Note-Taking

Oftentimes, when students are simply asked to take notes, they either write down everything in the text or nothing. They do the same with teacher lectures. We've found that students take the best notes when they are provided with structure. Many teachers use a simple two-column note-taking form. Keywords are written in the left column. Using those as prompts, students take notes in the right column. We added a third column with our students, adding a place for them to draw an image that would remind them of the information.

Another popular format for note-taking is Cornell Notes. The format provides a focus through the essential question, space for notes, and then a summary.

Cornell Notes

Topic / Objective:	Name:
	Class / Period:
	Date:

Essential Question:

Questions:	Notes:

Summary:

 Math-Aids.Com

Another alternative that is particularly helpful for students who respond to visual cues is mind mapping. Although we provide a sample below, we recommend that you allow students to be creative with this process, as long as they demonstrate learning.

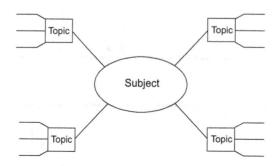

Writing Skills and Processes

It's not enough to simply expect students to write effectively. We need to teach them both the skills and the processes they need in order to be successful writers.

Writing Skills

Planning.
Communicating clearly.
Writing concisely.
Organizing ideas.
Constructing a logical argument.
Providing evidence and sources.
Elaborating with outside connections (to other texts, to themselves, to the real world).
Mechanics.

In order to teach writing skills, it's important to show samples of good writing, model what you want, allow students to practice in small groups, and then write independently.

Writing Processes

Students often assume that "good writers" simply write something and then are done. With the exception of short items such as exit slips, we need to incorporate teaching writing as a process. Although some teachers very the exact number of steps, these are typical activities that should occur as students write.

The Writing Process

Prewriting: During this step, students plan their writing. You can provide support through graphic organizers, providing reading or research materials, or giving students ideas through a classroom discussion.

Drafting: Have students write their "first stab" at their paper. Remind them that the purpose of this step is to get their thoughts on paper, and they should not worry about perfection.

Revising and Editing: Revision focuses on content; editing, on grammar and mechanics. During this portion of the writing process, you'll want to conference with students, provide for peer conferences, teach mini-lessons on specific issues, and allow for plenty of questions.

Rewriting: Have students incorporate changes as they carefully write or type their final drafts.

Publishing: Encourage students to publish their works in a variety of ways.

Increase Amount of Writing Time

It is also important to increase the overall amount of time that students spend writing in the classroom. Although this can be a formal writing lesson or a large project like a research paper, you can also incorporate writing in small ways throughout your lesson. Many of the other instructional suggestions we've already looked at, such as exit slips, require students to use writing to demonstrate learning. Others include writing letters or postcards to summarize information, keeping learning logs or journals, or working together for collaborative note-taking where each student in a group summarizes one section of the text and then students share information.

Suggestions for Incorporating Writing in Sample Subject Areas

Math	Science
One sentence explaining how students solved a problem.	Create a front page of a website or newspaper about the topic.
One sentence explaining why a student used a particular strategy.	Video responses.
Learning logs to review material.	Letters/blogs about science issues (pro/con).
Think-Write-Share.	Write hypotheses/procedures/results.
Alphabet book of math vocabulary.	Write about an alternative experiment that could measure a similar variable.

Art	Physical Education
Primary Grades:	Choose sport; list strengths and areas of improvement.
Draw an original creature; write sounds they make.	Develop action plan for improvement.
Draw a treasure map and write directions.	Keep a record and track progress.
Create and send thank-you stars to local veterans.	Create a job description for a specific category of athlete (runner, etc.).
Upper Grades:	
Make quilt paintings about goals and dreams; write an explanation.	
Design a building; write purpose and uses.	
Create own species; write about how it should be classified and explain.	

Which of the writing recommendations is strongest in your classroom? Which has room for improvement? What strategy would you like to try?

There are also several reading strategies to help students succeed.

Reading	
Recommendation	Source
Provide differentiated reading instruction based on assessment of reading levels.	Gersten and colleagues (2008).
Identify similarities and differences.	Marzano (2004).
Use cues and advance organizers.	Marzano (2004).

Differentiated Reading Instruction

Because students are working at different levels, we'll need to differentiate to maximize success. Differentiated instruction can be challenging to plan, but it is critical to enhance student learning.

Layering Meaning

With at-risk students, we have used a strategy called layering meaning to help them read and understand their social studies textbook. Because our students were reading below grade level, they struggled with our textbook. So, we found an article or section from another book on the same topic that was easier to read. Our students would read that material first, which helped them build background knowledge and learn some of the specialized vocabulary. Then, students returned to the main text and read it with our support. Since they had read the easier text, they were better able to handle the grade-level text, which is more rigorous. As your students progress through the year, some will no longer need the extra step. Others, however, will need the continued support.

Students who are more advanced start by reading the standard or grade-level text. Then, they read text that is written at a higher level for more advanced work. This lets you differentiate the reading assignments based on the skill level of your students. You will need to find text at varying levels for this strategy. There are commercial programs that provide this service, but Larry Ferlazzo, who writes a "Websites of the Day" blog (http://larry-ferlazzo.edublogs.org/about/), provides free online sources for leveled texts.

Grouping for Leveled Text

Teachers in one elementary school that we observed had a specific issue related to differentiation of content. About 75% of their students scored below grade level on state testing, and many were identified with learning disabilities. The fifth-grade teachers typically chose one novel for all of the students to read each month, but the novels were difficult for many students to read. The teachers wanted students to work at rigorous levels, but they also wanted them to be successful.

In February, the teachers wanted to read a biography of Martin Luther King Jr. Instead of choosing one book, they found four biographies at varying levels of readability. The students were then organized into groups based on their ability to read and discuss the novels. Each teacher met with one of the four groups to facilitate discussions and ensure understanding. Students who needed additional support received it during tier 2 or 3 instruction. Then, the students returned to their original classrooms, and all of the teachers led whole-group discussions about Martin Luther King Jr.

A key element of this process was that each of the books contained some information that the other groups had not read. During the class discussion, the teachers asked questions to elicit specific information from each group. One of the benefits was that even students in the lowest reading group had information to contribute to the discussion, reinforcing everyone's importance to the group. Students who could read at a higher level were challenged to do so. Finally, students were placed into new groups with others who had read different books so that they could create a final project about Martin Luther King Jr.

Other Ideas

The Access Center, which was a national technical assistance center funded by the Office of Special Education Programs within the Department of Education, wrote an article for Reading Rockets describing a variety of other ideas for differentiating reading instruction, especially based on readiness (www.readingrockets.org/article/differentiated-instruction-reading). We find these particularly helpful.

Strategy	Focus of Differen- tiation	Definition	Example
Tiered Assignments	Readiness	Tiered assignments are designed to instruct students on essential skills that are provided at different levels of complexity, abstractness, and open-endedness. The curricular content and objective(s) are the same, but the process and/or product are varied according to the student's level of readiness.	Students with moderate comprehension skills are asked to create a story web. Students with advanced comprehension skills are asked to retell a story from the point of view of the main character.

(Continued)

(Continued)

Compacting	Readiness	Compacting is the process of adjusting instruction to account for prior student mastery of learning objectives. Compacting involves a three-step process: assess the student to determine his or her level of knowledge on the material to be studied and determine what he or she still needs to master; create plans for what the student needs to know, and excuse the student from studying what he or she already knows; and create plans for freed-up time to be spent in enriched or accelerated study.	A student who can decode words with short vowel sounds would not participate in a direct instruction lesson for that skill but might be provided with small-group or individualized instruction on a new phonics skill.
Interest Centers or Interest Groups	Readiness, interest	Interest centers (usually used with younger students) and interest groups (usually used with older students) are set up so that learning experiences are directed toward a specific learner interest. Allowing students to choose a topic can be motivating to them.	**Interest Centers:** Centers can focus on specific reading skills, such as phonics or vocabulary, and provide examples and activities that center on a theme of interest, such as outer space or students' favorite cartoon characters. **Interest Groups:** For a book report, students can work in interest groups with other students who want to read the same book.

Flexible Grouping	Readiness, interest, learning profile	Students work as part of many different groups, depending on the task and/or content. Sometimes, students are placed in groups based on readiness; other times, they are placed based on interest and/or learning profile. Groups can either be assigned by the teacher or chosen by the students. Students can be assigned purposefully to a group or assigned randomly. This strategy allows students to work with a wide variety of peers and keeps them from being labeled as advanced or struggling.	The teacher may assign groups based on readiness for phonics instruction while allowing other students to choose their own groups for book reports, based on the book topic.
Learning Contracts	Readiness, learning profile	Learning contracts begin with an agreement between the teacher and the student. The teacher specifies the necessary skills expected to be learned by the student and the required components of the assignment, and the student identifies methods for completing the tasks. This strategy: 1. allows students to work at an appropriate pace; 2. can target learning styles; and 3. helps students work independently, learn planning skills, and eliminate unnecessary skill practice.	A student indicates that he or she wants to research a particular author. With support from the teacher, the student determines how the research will be conducted and how the information will be presented to the class. For example, the student might decide to write a paper and present a poster to the class. The learning contract indicates the dates by which each step of the project will be completed.

(Continued)

(Continued)

| Choice Boards | Readiness, interest, learning profile | Choice boards are organizers that contain a variety of activities. Students can choose one or several activities to complete as they learn a skill or develop a product.

Choice boards can be organized so that students are required to choose options that focus on several different skills. | After students read *Romeo and Juliet*, they are given a choice board that contains a list of possible activities for each of the following learning styles: visual, auditory, kinesthetic, and tactile. Students must complete two activities from the board and must choose these activities from two different learning styles. |

In terms of differentiating instruction (including the concept of layering meaning), which idea would you like to try?

Similarities and Differences

Comparing and contrasting information is a common classroom activity. Two frequently used graphic organizers for that purpose are T-charts and Venn diagrams.

Semantic Feature Analysis

There are a variety of other ways to teach similarities and differences. A semantic feature analysis is a cross chart that works well to compare characteristics or features. Students mark the columns that apply to each row and then discuss the similarities and differences.

Topic 1	*Topic 2*

Polygon Feature Analysis

		Forced Choices				
	Convex	Equi-lateral	Equi-angular	4-Sided	3-Sided	Opposite Sides Parallel
Square						
Rectangle						
Triangle						
Quadrilateral						
Regular Polygon						
Rhombus						
Trapezoid						

Forced choices are questions that require students to choose a side and explain their choice.

Examples of Forced Choices

Would you rather go to school only for four months in the winter and have the rest of the year off or go to school in the summer and have the rest of the year off?

Would you rather live in Narnia or go to school at Hogwarts?

Would you rather save your country from an invasion or from a terrible disease?

Would you rather be a teacher at your school or the principal?

Would you rather be a researcher or the owner of a drug company?

Would you rather lose your ability to speak or have to say everything you are thinking?

Would you rather be an author or an illustrator?

Would you rather be an obtuse angle or an acute angle?

Forced-choice questions are an excellent way to prompt discussion on similarities and differences. Practice with these types of questions also builds skills needed for debates, which are also a rigorous, engaging way to showcase a student's knowledge of similarities and differences.

Two-Voice Poems

A creative way to compare and contrast two concepts is a two-voice poem. Ask students to list what they know about each concept. Then, ask them to write some sample comments that each person or perspective might say. Next, students turn that into a poem of two voices by writing the comments as a back-and-forth conversation. Before you decide this is only a language arts activity, look at the example developed by Ben Lovelace, a physical education teacher, to demonstrate the different roles of two basketball players.

Point Guard	*Defender*
I'm the star of the show.	*I can steal it, you know.*
I'm the leader of the pack.	*I'm the one to keep you back.*
I'll let my shots fall like rain.	*I'm the one who wins the games.*
I can take you to the basket with my muscle.	*I'll beat you there with my hustle.*

Cues and Advance Organizers

Cues and advance organizers help prepare students for the content they will be learning. One of the most common advance organizers is a KWL chart. However, there are other ways to help students get ready to learn, including anticipation guides.

Directions: Tell whether the statement is true or false.

_____1. The longest side of a triangle is called the hypotenuse.
_____2. In the Pythagorean theorem, the variable c stands for the hypotenuse.
_____3. In a right triangle, the sides that meet at the right angle are called legs.
_____4. A corollary is a statement that can be easily proved using other proofs.
_____5. If you know the lengths of all three sides of a triangle, you can use the Pythagorean theorem to determine whether it is a right triangle.

Anticipation Organizing Guides

One type of metacognitive modeling is to provide an advanced organizer for students. An anticipation guide is particularly helpful. In this case, it is used during reading to help students process their thinking.

Topic: _____

K What I Know	W What I Want to Know	L What I Have Learned

Anticipation guides can be used in any subject area.

Anticipation Guide

Read each of the following statements. Then decide how strongly you agree or disagree with each. Explain your thinking in a sentence or two.

SA = Strongly Agree	A = Agree				D = Disagree	SD = Strongly Disagree

Statements	SA	A	D	SD	Explanations

After reading/discussing, look back at your ratings and explanations. Discuss how your thinking has changed or been confirmed on one or more of the statements.

Source: www.readwritethink.org/files/resources/printouts/AnticipationGuide.pdf

Math Prior Knowledge Anticipation Guide

You can also use anticipation guides to determine what a student actually understands about a concept prior to instruction. Pat Vining, a math teacher, uses a simple activity to check her students' prior knowledge of the concept and to clear up any misunderstandings students may have about the topic. First, she gives students three minutes to answer a short true-false questionnaire. Next, in pairs, students compare responses and use the textbook to check their answers. Each set of partners must rewrite any false statements so that they are true. She ends with a whole-class discussion to ensure understanding.

Pythagorean Theorem

Topic or Chapter/Text		
True-False Questions	*My Answer*	*Correct Answer and Where I Found the Information*

Adapted from: www.readingrockets.org/strategies/anticipation_guide/

Characteristics of Effective Anticipation Guides

Ausubel, Novak, and Hanesian (1978) describe a structured anticipatory guide. As you plan the guide, keep in mind the following steps. Additionally, students must be taught how to use the guide throughout their task.

Effective Anticipation Guides

Inform the students of the use of an advance organizer.
Identify the major topics and tasks.
Provide an organizational framework.
Clarify the action to be taken or completed.
Provide background information.
State concepts to be learned.
Clarify concepts to be learned.
Motivate students to learn through establishing relevance. Introduce and identify new vocabulary.
State general outcomes and objectives to be mastered.

Have you ever used an anticipation guide? Based on the recommendations and examples, how can you use one to help your students learn?

Vocabulary

Vocabulary	
Recommendation	*Source*
Teach spelling patterns.	Scammacca and colleagues (2007).
Improve knowledge of word meaning and concepts (especially adolescents); teach content area vocabulary.	Scammacca and colleagues (2007); Marzano (2004).

Spelling Patterns

Sample Strategies for Teaching Spelling Patterns
Phonetic spelling. Vowel rules. Consonant patterns. Syllabication rules. Morphemic strategies (roots, affixes, etc.). Rhyming patterns.

Activities to Play With Words and Spelling Patterns

Picture Books

Choose a picture book that reflects the spelling pattern you want to reinforce. For example, if you want to teach vowel sounds, choose a book such as *The Vowel Family: A Tale of Lost Letters* by Sally M. Walker. After reading the book (either as a read-aloud, a shared selection, or independently), revisit the text, identifying the vowel sounds. Then, play a game of Finding the Lost Vowels, where students find vowels in other books.

Three Alike/Red Herring

Barbara sometimes wondered what her students would learn if she didn't package everything together for them. One day, instead of telling them the pattern for spelling words, she decided to let them figure it out. She named multiple words: *ball*, *boy*, and *basket*. After a few seconds, one student shouted, "Hey, I know—those all begin with *b*!" This is an easy way to determine what students already know, and it can be used with any pattern.

To increase the rigor, Lindsay Yearta uses the Red Herring game with her students. She gives multiple examples that are linked, but students must identify the red herring—the one that does *not* belong. They must also justify their choice. Again, based on their responses, you can see how much they know, and by shifting the focus to students generating information, it is more rigorous.

StairSteps

In StairSteps, students are given an initial consonant or vowel. Then, they add one letter to try to create a word. They pass their paper to the next person, who adds another letter. This continues until there is a completed word. Whoever ends up with the completed word writes a sentence with the word. Note that some students will finish earlier, as some words will be shorter.

Manipulating Letters

In manipulating letters, students are given a spelling or vocabulary word. Then, they make a list of words that are within that word. For example, *square* includes words such as *are* and *sea*.

Word Meaning and Concepts/Content Area Vocabulary

Janet Allen's Academic Vocabulary

In *Tools for Teaching Academic Vocabulary*, Janet Allen organized academic vocabulary by context. She explained there are four types of words: general academic words, domain- or discipline-specific terms, topic-specific vocabulary, and passage-critical words.

Four Types of Academic Vocabulary

General academic vocabulary.
Domain- or discipline-specific vocabulary.
Topic-specific vocabulary.
Passage-critical vocabulary.

First, there is general academic vocabulary, which is not discipline-specific. Students frequently see these words, such as *analyze, synthesize, contrast,* and *restate.* It's important to provide detailed instruction on these words with lots of practice so that students are very familiar with them.

Next, Allen described domain- or discipline-specific words, which are frequently used within a specific discipline such as science or math. These words include terms such as *foreshadowing, hypothesis, rational number,* or *aerobic exercise.* Within the content area, these words should be reinforced regularly.

Third, there are topic-specific words. They are needed to understand a specific lesson or topic and are typically critical to an understanding of the concept. Direct instruction is usually necessary with these terms. Examples include *Holocaust, biome,* and *impressionism.*

Finally, passage-critical words are those that are necessary to understand a specific text. These words are crucial to comprehension of the passage. Particularly for specialized words, direct instruction is needed. Janet explained that in the book *Bats: Biggest! Littlest!* by Sandra Markle, sample passage-critical words include *echolocation, horning, roost,* and *wingspan.*

Thinking about the different types of vocabulary will help content area teachers explore words in a more meaningful way, as opposed to having students simply memorize definitions of random word lists.

Strategies for Teaching Vocabulary

Now let's look at seven strategies for teaching and reinforcing vocabulary.

Vocabulary Strategies

Visuals.
Word logs and word walls.
Multiple-meaning words.
Mnemonics.
Possible sentences.
Games.

Using Visuals to Enhance Understanding

Visuals can help students understand new concepts. We were in a social studies classroom in which the teacher was presenting geography terms such as *equator, latitude,* and *longitude.* She drew a circle on the board to illustrate Earth, and then she wrote the word *equator* across the center. She wrote the word *latitude* horizontally from west to east where the latitude lines go across Earth. Finally, she wrote the word *longitude* from north to south to clearly illustrate the meaning of the word. She provided visual context for her students as they encountered the terms for the first time.

In *Rigor Is Not a Four-Letter Word*, Barbara shared a graphic organizer to help students demonstrate their understanding in ways that required them to synthesize information about a term or concept and refine it down to the key points. Using the graphic organizer, students discuss different elements of a particular vocabulary term.

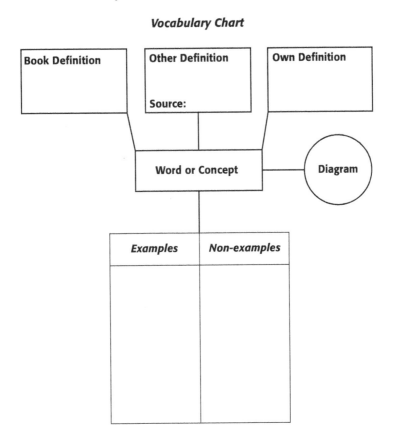

Vocabulary Chart

Then, students could create their own graphic organizers to take notes about and demonstrate their understanding of vocabulary. We remember one student bringing us a graphic organizer she had completed about the Pythagorean theorem. She had used right triangles to organize the information. Using visuals helps students connect their learning.

Word Logs and Word Walls

Many teachers use word walls, or sections of a bulletin board or wall to display vocabulary terms. Effective word walls are incorporated into instruction, rather than simply being a list of words posted on the wall. One adaptation we saw is to use larger pieces of paper that are folded in half. On the outside of the paper, list the word. Students can flip the cover up to see a picture and a sentence for the word. We like this because the sentence puts the word in context, and the picture is a visual cue.

Another alternative is for students to collect personal logs or dictionaries. This can be a portion of a notebook or a folder with sticky notes of various words. We were in a primary classroom where students used coat hangers with words dangling from string as their own dictionaries. The final product isn't important; what matters is providing students a way to keep up with their own list of words.

Multiple-Meaning Words

Particularly in specific content areas, it's important to teach words that have multiple meanings. Barbara was observing a student teacher in a science classroom one day, and he asked, "Does anyone know what *grounded* means?" It was his opening question for a lesson on electricity. Immediately, one student shouted out, "That's what happened to me last week when I made a C on my test!" Everyone laughed, but that's an excellent example of a multiple-meaning word. We need to specifically teach students the different meanings of these words. Janet Allen shared a chart that helps.

It Fits
Identify the term (including pronunciation). Tell the definition. Find a keyword that sounds like the term. Imagine the keyword doing something with the term (drawing). Think about this interaction. Study until you know it.

Keyword Mnemonics

Richard T. Boon and Vicky G. Spencer, in their book *Adolescent Literacy: Strategies for Content Comprehension in Inclusive Classrooms*, shared that students with disabilities can benefit from using mnemonics. They provide a specific example, It Fits, originally developed to teach science vocabulary and definitions.

In math, you can review mathematics word problems based on their underlying structure rather than keywords (Gersten et al., 2009). These structures are known as schema-based problem solving. Common structures are Group, Difference, and Change types. To use schema-based problem solving, students read the word, determine the problem type, input quantities to the associated graphic organizer, solve the problem, and make sense of the answer. A mnemonic that may be used with schema-based problem solving is RIPPEM.

RIPPEM

Read and understand the problem.
Identify the schema.
Put together the diagram.
Plug in the numbers appropriately.
Establish the equation and answer.
Make sure the answer makes sense.

Possible Sentences

Possible Sentences is a relatively simple strategy for teaching word meanings and generating class discussion. It also sparks interest from students and uses analysis skills. The authors at All About Adolescent Literacy (adlit. org) describe the process.

1. Before students read the text, visually display the chosen vocabulary.
2. Ask students to define the words and pair related words together.
3. Ask individuals or pairs of students to write sentences using their word pairs. Remind students that their sentences should be ones they expect to see in the text as they read.
4. Have students read the text and compare their possible sentences with the actual sentences within the text.
5. If your students' possible sentences are inaccurate, ask them to rewrite their sentences to be accurate.
6. Invite students to share their sentences with the class.

Playing Games

We need to experience new words and concepts multiple times in a variety of ways. Too often, we expect students to fully understand a word after they have read it one time. However, reading a word multiple times doesn't ensure understanding, either. Your students need to play with words in fun and different ways to help them learn.

During Headband, Erin writes a word on a sentence strip and makes it into a headband. First-graders in her class give clues to the person wearing the headband, who must guess the word. All students are involved, and the activity encourages her students to learn from each other.

James Good, a middle school drama teacher, points out that his students find the language of Shakespearean plays challenging. For key scenes, students are broken into groups with five acting parts and a group director. He explains:

> Students identify difficult turns of phrase or specific vocabulary words and make their best educated guess as to meaning. They run lines with one another to improve pronunciation and dramatic reading. The director makes suggestions as to simple stage movements that can be done in the small space at the front of the room. The group discusses appropriate tone, body language, and facial expression. Concerning themselves with the dramatic aspects of presenting to the other three groups more or less forces them to make meaning. Each group takes a turn in a kind of "drama slam." They try to outdo the others and get delightfully hammy.

Which vocabulary strategy have you used in your classroom? Which would you like to try?

Conclusion

Literacy is a crucial lifelong skill. Reading and writing at rigorous levels is infused into every aspect of our daily lives. Research-based strategies for literacy, especially for reading and writing, will help all students learn at high levels.

6

Rigorous Assessment in the RTI/MTSS Classroom

Assessment is often considered the backbone of MTSS because instructional and curricular decisions are based on data. Making informed decisions requires a number of assessments that must be balanced so that they focus on effective approaches without stealing unnecessary instructional time. We must also ensure that we do not water down rigorous assessments. The goal of an MTSS program is to hold all students to the same high expectations while providing the support students need in order to be successful.

Multiple types of assessments are used in an MTSS approach: screening, progress monitoring, and diagnostics.

> Screening, progress monitoring, and diagnostic assessments drive the vast majority of our framework. However, we do look at other formative and outcome-based data. We also look at different data, such as "office discipline referrals" for behavior.
>
> Todd Wiedemann, Assistant Director of Kansas MTSS (2016)

Screening	Diagnostic	Progress Monitoring
Determines tier	Determines instruction	Adjust and adapt

Timeline for Assessments

Minimal expectations are the use of a screener at least twice yearly, diagnostics quarterly, and progress monitoring or benchmark assessment at least quarterly. However, it should be noted that a higher frequency of assessments is beneficial to intervention selection.

Minimum Expectations							
Assessment Timeline Academic Year							
Fall Screener				Winter Screener			
Diagnostic		Diagnostic		Diagnostic		Diagnostic	
Quarterly Benchmark		Quarterly Benchmark		Quarterly Benchmark		Quarterly Benchmark	
Progress Monitor	Progress Monitor	Progress Monitor	Progress Monitor	Progress Monitor	Progress Monitor	Progress Monitor	Progress Monitor

Initial Assessment: Screening and Placement

As we saw in the yearly calendar, the first recommendation from both the reading and math RTI/MTSS practice guides from the Institute of Education Sciences (Gersten et al., 2008; Gersten et al., 2009) is to screen all students for potential mathematics or reading problems at the beginning and middle of the academic year.

Data from universal screeners such as DIBELS, easyCBM and AIM-Sweb are the primary data source for examining the health of the core and instructional decision-making for Tier 1 practices, and identifying students in need of [support]. Other data such as student achievement outcome measures (i.e., state tests) and assessment in formation from the curriculum and teacher-developed formative assessments may also be used at this level.

Oregon Response to Intervention and Instruction (2016)

When it comes to assigning the appropriate tier for students, the percentage score on the screening instruments often determines these decisions. One way to place students is to look at a school's data and identify the lowest academic performing 20%. Of the lowest 20%, the lowest 5% receive tier 3 intervention. The remaining 15% receive tier 2 intervention. Students who scored between 21% and 25% but are not receiving tier 2 intervention would be identified for the respective core classroom teacher to provide additional supports in the tier 1 setting.

Sample Tier Placement by School Percentages		
Screening Score Percentage 0–5%	Screening Score Percentage 6–20%	Screening Score Percentage 21–25%
Tier 3 services	Tier 2 services	Tier 1 services

Decision-Making Process

Rather than setting specific percentages, you can also use ranges. It is important to consider a flowchart of decision-making to guide the intervention placement and adjustment process. The review process below provides a method for determining services, as well as shaping future assessment timelines.

Based on the student's performance on the screening measure, the MTSS team decides whether or not the student performs at a minimal level of expectation. If not, then the student receives a necessary level of intervention within the required range. The lower the scores, the more intensive the level of intervention. Likewise, if the student scores exceptionally high on the screener, then acceleration programs should be considered. Students who scored low on the screener and especially those receiving intervention should have their progress monitored in their respective areas of need. Progress monitoring data should be reviewed frequently to verify and adjust levels of intervention intensity that most appropriately meet the needs of the student.

Funding as an Issue

Although setting clear and specific guidelines makes the decision process easier, it may not be the most appropriate. You may have a larger group that needs intensive tier 3 intervention, or there may be 20% of the school population that requires tier 2 intervention. In such cases, funding becomes a major barrier. In several school districts, money is split proportionally by population numbers rather than needs. For example, in one middle school, nearly 50% of the students are performing at Basic or Below Basic levels. Meanwhile, on the other side of town, 20% are performing at Basic or Below Basic. However, the local district may provide funding simply based on a per-pupil basis, without accounting for the different needs. In such cases, the district and school board should consider allocating appropriate funding to support the students who need the MTSS approach the most. Hiring more interventionists for the school with the highest need is a logical decision, but one that often requires longer and sometimes more heated discussions with the community.

Review screening data and set cutpoints

Significantly low scores or untestable	Lower than cutscores	Within cutscore range	Higher than cutscores	Significantly high scores
Consider Tier 3 and special education evaluation	Provide a diagnostic and consider Tier 2	Monitor progress and review at future date	Hold and review after next screening	Consider accelerated gifted program
Monitor progress in both core and intervention		Monitor progress in core		
if progress is satisfactory, then consider Tier 2 supports.	if progress is satisfactory, then consider Tier 1 differentiation only.	If progress is satisfactory, then fade supports, as appropriate.	If progress is satisfactory, then maintain instruction.	If progress is satisfactory, then maintain.
if progress is not satisfactory, then consider placement in special education.	if progress is not satisfactory, then adjust intervention and consider Tier 3.	if progress is not satisfactory, then adjust supports and consider Tier 2.	If progress is not satisfactory, then consider supports, as appropriate.	If progress is not satisfactory, then consider core instruction.

Logistical concerns influence our decisions. Which of these has impacted your program? Did you learn something new that will help you?

Screening Tools for Placement

There are a variety of sources for appropriate screening tools. Often, your state or district will mandate the screening tools. Most are commercial and generic, but they have been validated. Validity and reliability are particularly important because the screener is designed to predict how students will perform on statewide high-stakes tests.

Characteristics of Universal Screening Assessments

Accessible to all students.

Assess critical skills and concepts.

Brief (under 15 minutes), easy to administer and score.

Given to all students (i.e., district, school, grade level, course).

Quick turnaround time (1–3 days) of aggregated and disaggregated data to classroom teachers.

Repeatable.

Reliable (Commercial assessments have undergone psychometric analyses to determine reliability. A "teacher-made" assessment cannot be referred to as reliable if it has not been analyzed by a psychometrician.).

Valid (Commercial assessments have undergone psychometric analyses to determine validity. The inferences made from a "teacher-made" assessment cannot be referred to as valid, if it has not been analyzed by a psychometrician.).

Source: www.sde.ct.gov/sde/lib/sde/pdf/curriculum/cali/elementary_assessments_4-9-12.pdf

---

Diagnostic Assessment

Determining the appropriate tier for students is only the first step. In order to determine the area needed for intervention, a screening isn't enough. Further assessment must be done to determine areas of need.

Such assessments are diagnostics designed to determine areas of strengths and needs. Screening determines who is struggling or succeeding, whereas diagnostics point more precisely to the reasons why.

Screening	Diagnostics
Determines who is struggling or succeeding.	Determine why there is a struggle.

Diagnostics are typically completed in the core setting based on performance in the core curriculum. Diagnostic assessments may be purchased, such as a Woodcock-Johnson or a KeyMath assessment. On a more formative level, teachers can develop these diagnostics in their classrooms.

Sample Commercial Diagnostic Tools	Sample Teacher-Developed Diagnostic Tools
Woodcock-Johnson. Qualitative Reading Inventory (free online ones: https://teachers.net/mentors/remedial_reading/topic2804/9.01.12.09.42.42.html). KeyMath-3. Iowa Test of Basic Skills (ITBS). Diagnostic Assessments of Reading (DAR).	Running records. Reading inventories. Error pattern analysis. Diagnostic task analysis. Conceptual rubrics. Procedural checklists.

Let's look at two samples, one in reading and one in math. However, each of these can also be used in the other subject area with adaptations.

Running Records

In reading, running records have been used for several decades. Using a running record, a teacher determines why a student is struggling. Running records are assessments completed while a student is working in order to determine more precise details about their learning. The notes a teacher makes are based on his or her observations of the student's performance.

Sample Running Record		
Student reads: Suzie walked to the store with her brother.		
Teacher marks on her copy: X √ √ √ √ √ X X Suzie walked to the store with her brother.		
Errors noted:	Difficulty with /er/ sound	Short vowel sound in /Suzie/
Notes:	Appeared nervous and was hesitant before errors occurred. In grade-level passage, read 35 words per minute.	

Based on this diagnostic, if this was typical of the student's performance, intervention would focus on /er/ sounds and reading fluency. For upper grades, the process is the same but uses more challenging text. Although running records are not typically used in math classrooms, you can modify them to note errors in problem solving and to look for patterns.

Diagnostic Task Analysis

As content becomes more complex, the potential for increased errors makes error pattern analysis more complex. In such cases, it is important to analyze the tasks used in an approach to an outcome and assess based on that task analysis. In the following example, a Cincinnati teacher task analyzed multi-digit multiplication (two digits by two digits) and performed a diagnostic on a small group. If this were typical behavior of each student, three of the students need intervention in multiplication fact accuracy and fluency, and three others need intervention to accurately line up their partial products. You'll also note how easily this can be adapted to reading and writing.

Sample Math Task Analysis Diagnostic

	Multi fact	*Combo*	*Carry in*	*Carry out*	*Add carry*	*Line up products*	*Add facts*	*Answer*
Johnny Fever	X	√	√	√	√	√	√	X
Les Nessman	√	√	√	√	√	√	√	√
Andy Travis	√	√	√	√	√	X	√	X

A potential roadblock of quick diagnostics is that careless errors are generalized. Occasional errors may be due to carelessness. However, when similar errors are made across multiple problems, these errors are considered patterns. Such concerns should be handled in core classes or during intervention.

> What type of diagnostic assessment(s) do you currently use? Are any of these suggestions new ideas?

Ongoing Progress Monitoring

Progress monitoring is a frequent incremental assessment of student performance, which provides an important tool for MTSS teams. There is no perfect instructional approach or program, so it is important to continuously evaluate student performance based on the interventions selected. Progress monitoring provides teachers an "eyeball" way of doing just that.

Progress monitoring has one of the largest effects on student performance (Hattie, Masters, & Birch, 2015).

> When teachers use CBM information to monitor student progress and make instructional changes in response to student data, students achieve significantly more than do students whose teachers use their own assessment practices.
>
> (Stecker, Lembke, & Foegen, 2008, p. 49)

> Progress monitoring encompasses a system of brief assessments that are given frequently, at least monthly, to determine whether students are progressing through the curriculum in desired fashion and are likely to meet long-term goals.
>
> (Stecker, Fuchs, & Fuchs, 2008, p. 11)

Progress Monitoring Process

Stecker, Lembke, and Foegen (2008) suggested a five-step process when using progress monitoring:

1. Select Appropriate Materials: Select materials that match the construct of student need. If interested in purchasing a progress monitoring program, see the National Center on Intensive Intervention (www.intensiveintervention.org/chart/progress-monitoring). To create progress monitoring probes (1 to 5-minute brief assessments), you can do so on www.interventioncentral.org/curriculum-based-measurement-reading-math-assesment-tests. You can follow the same process with a reading passage of 140–200 words to compute oral reading fluency of middle-level students.

Example of a Probe Used for Progress Monitoring

Student Name: _____ Date:_____ Target Skill: Lowercase Consonant Letter Naming

Total Correct____ Total Errors____ Skipped____ Notes_____

l	x	d	q	t	r	c	f	z	m	p	j	__/12: 12
n	s	k	w	y	v	b	f	t	h	v	j	__/12: 24
s	m	c	k	l	p	n	x	r	z	g	b	__/12: 36
q	y	d	w	k	f	y	h	j	r	x	s	__/12: 48
t	w	c	v	z	q	m	p	l	n	b	g	__/12: 60
d	m	n	c	d	t	p	r	y	s	k	v	__/12: 72
q	z	x	l	j	f	g	h	w	b	j	p	__/12: 84

Witzel's Computation Probes   Multiplication/Division   09
Mixed signs of products but not all in parentheses

$-3(^+9)$	$-8(-2)$	$\dfrac{^+15}{3}$	$-3(-8)$
$\dfrac{-27}{(-3)}$	$9(-5)$	$(^+5)8$	$\dfrac{(-10)}{^+2}$
$(^+8)2$	$\dfrac{(^+35)}{-5}$	$\dfrac{-21}{(^+3)}$	$-5(^+6)$
$-3(-6)$	$(8)(-5)$	$\dfrac{-28}{4}$	$(^+3)9$
$\dfrac{(^+24)}{6}$	$\dfrac{-24}{(-3)}$	$(-4)6$	$4(-8)$
$(-14)2$	$\dfrac{-16}{(^+4)}$	$-1(^+3)$	$\dfrac{(^+32)}{-8}$
$\dfrac{-14}{(-7)}$	$(^+2)-6$	$\dfrac{-18}{(^+9)}$	$\dfrac{(^+24)}{3}$
$3(^+8)$	$\dfrac{-20}{(-5)}$	$\dfrac{-12}{(^+3)}$	$5(-9)$
$-2(^+4)$	$\dfrac{(^+24)}{-4}$	$\dfrac{(^+12)}{3}$	$(-5)-7$
$3(^+8)$	$(^+2)6$	$\dfrac{(-28)}{-4}$	$4(-4)$
$\dfrac{-32}{(^+4)}$	$\dfrac{18}{(^+3)}$	$(-6)5$	$2(-8)$
$-5(-8)$	$\dfrac{16}{(-4)}$	$(-3)7$	$\dfrac{(-28)}{-7}$

2. Evaluate Technical Features: Examine the features of the curriculum-based measurement probes so that they truly assess the construct with some sense of reliability and validity. In the first example on the preceding page, make sure that if we are working on letter naming of consonants, this is exactly what the student needs to develop and this skill will also help improve the student's performance in the standards-based core.

3. Administer and Score Measures: Check to make certain that every person who administers the assessment does so equally, in what is referred to as interrater reliability. Importantly, include the student in the scoring. Show the student what was successful and share obvious error patterns. Let students graph their performance, both correct answers and errors, so that they can see growth as they improve in their performance. There are few better ways to motivate a student than to show success.

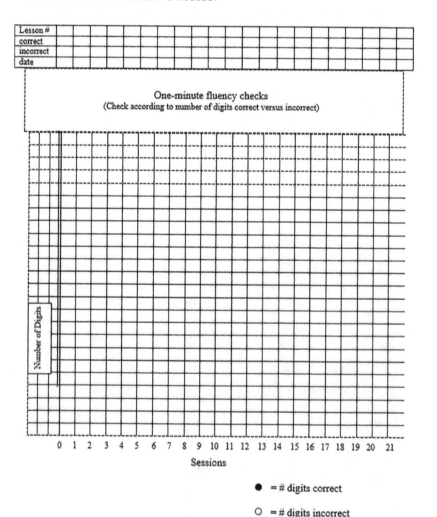

4. Use Data for Goal Setting: Use early scores to set a baseline to determine the level at which the student is performing. Then, set the desired goal that should occur by the end of the intervention. For example, if a student should be reading 120 words per minute and the planned intervention lasts 15 weeks, then at week 15 in the invention, there should be an *x* marked and a line from the baseline score to the *x*. This line is called the goal line. The goal line shows how well a student is expected to progress from where they started to later points in the intervention. Involve the student in this conversation so that he or she knows what is expected.

What progress monitoring measures do you use? How well do these measures connect to the students' deficit areas and core content needs?

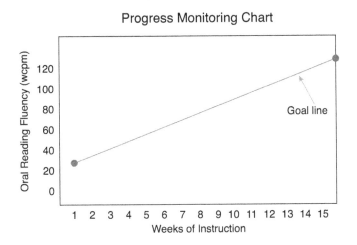

Progress Monitoring Chart

5. Judge Instructional Effectiveness: The student's work reveals the trend in their performance. Student data from progress monitoring should be graphed to better judge the intervention for its effectiveness. Aptly called a trend line, the slope of the trend line indicates whether or not the child is learning. A positive slope shows positive growth while a negative slope shows the student is performing worse. However, don't think that a positive slope means that the intervention is wholly successful.

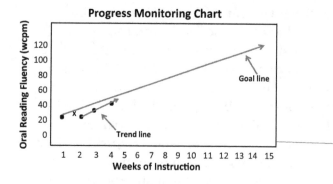

In this example, the student's performance is a positive slope. However, in this example, the trend line is coming closer to the goal line each week revealing that the student is doing better and will likely meet her goal before the end of the intervention. So, this is a successful intervention.

Successful Intervention

The student's trend line, performance, should approach the goal line.

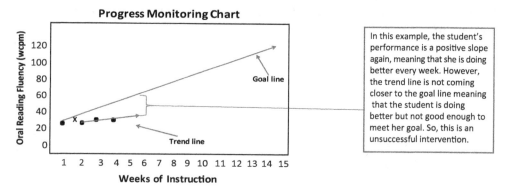

In this example, the student's performance is a positive slope again, meaning that she is doing better every week. However, the trend line is not coming closer to the goal line meaning that the student is doing better but not good enough to meet her goal. So, this is an unsuccessful intervention.

Unsuccessful Intervention

An unsuccessful intervention would show an increasing gap between the trend and goal lines.

How would it affect the student to track his or her own data and goal line?

Progress Monitoring in the Core: Benchmark Assessments

Progress monitoring should occur frequently for students in intervention settings. Although it is critical to determine how well students are performing on their deficit skills during intervention, it is also important to determine if working on this deficit is helping improve their understanding of the standards-based core instruction. In order to determine this, we need to assess growth in the tier 1 or core setting. A benchmark assessment should be developed based on the standards that were taught, at least quarterly. In other words, in an eighth-grade pre-algebra course, near the end of the first quarter, a quarterly assessment must be administered that covers the standards taught. Sometimes districts provide benchmarks, and oftentimes textbooks include quarterly benchmarks. However, in many cases, a grade-level or course-level team must develop their own, particularly if they aren't using a textbook or they have a unit/curriculum guide that doesn't tackle a textbook sequentially. Such benchmarks may be developed by sampling a few key curriculum items from the quarter. When doing so, we suggest making the benchmark assessment brief so that the construct is the curriculum and not the student's test endurance.

When you are designing your own benchmarks, you want to match the content, but they also need to be high quality, including a level of rigor. In Barbara's book *Rigor and Assessment in the Classroom*, she provided information on several types of questions, along with tips for writing quality items.

Frequently Used Question Types

Matching.
True-false.
Fill-in-the-blank.
Multiple-choice.
Short-answer.

Matching Questions

Matching questions are an easy, quick way to assess a wide of range student knowledge. However, it is difficult to assess at a higher level of rigor, as most matching tests measure basic recall questions. Depending on the items, students can guess at the correct answer rather than truly demonstrating understanding.

What are the best strategies for developing quality matching tests? First, make sure there is one best option for each item you list. Ensure that students can see why the items match, so that there is clear evidence that students understand the link. Also, provide more examples than items that match them. For example, if you have a list of vocabulary terms and then definitions, add one or two extra definitions to increase the rigor.

One specific type of matching test can increase rigor: the expanded matching format, which creates three columns to be matched. It provides a better opportunity to measure what students know. In this case, you'll also notice that there are more choices than items, which requires students to narrow down the answer.

Women's Historical Contributions		
Person	*Contribution*	*Decade*
A. Fannie Lou Hamer. B. Shirley Chisolm. C. Marie Curie. D. Alice Paul.	1. U.S. Civil Rights activist and wife of Martin Luther King Jr. 2. Ran for state senate on the platform of increasing minority employment. 3. First African American member of Congress. 4. Discovered the elements radium and polonium. 5. Formed the Congressional Union (later named the National Women's Party) to raise public awareness for women's rights as a part of the woman suffragist movement. 6. Known as "Moses" and led many slaves to freedom along the Underground Railroad.	7. 1800s 8. 1910s 9. 1920s 10. 1950s 11. 1960s 12. 1970s

True-False Tests

True-false tests are an excellent way for students to determine the accuracy of a statement, agree with opinions, and define terms. As with matching items, these are graded quickly and easily, and students can answer a wide range of questions in a short amount of time. However, once again, questions are typically low-level recall questions, and you may not be sure whether students understand the question or are simply guessing. To combat this, and to increase the rigor, require students to rewrite any statements in false choices as true statements, which does require them to demonstrate a true understanding of the content.

In order to create effective true-false questions, it's important to avoid trivial statements and focus on core instructional content. Statements should be detailed enough that students must thoroughly read them, rather than glancing down to make a quick decision. Also, if your statement includes an opinion, provide the source for clarity and correctness.

Tips for Writing True-False Tests

Use precise writing.
Be sure choices are absolutely true or false (no in-betweens).
Avoid *always*, *never*, *none*, and *all*.
Keep all statements approximately equal in length.
Don't reflect a pattern (T, F, T, F . . .).
Put T/F for students to circle so you don't have to guess at handwriting.
Avoid negative statements.

Fill-in-the-Blank Questions

Fill-in-the-blank questions are also used to assess basic levels of knowledge. These are typically sentences with a blank, and students must fill in one or more words to complete it. As with matching and true-false tests, they are fairly easy to grade and they don't take much time to create. It is very difficult to find a way to make these questions rigorous. However, they do have their place, as long as you limit the use of these questions.

When creating a fill-in-the-blank question, be sure that your omitted words are critical to the content of the sentence. Otherwise, you end up with too many choices, and your students don't demonstrate understanding of the content.

One specific type of fill-in-the-blank item that is helpful, particularly for reading content (including content area reading), is the cloze model. With this method, you provide students a text to read, generally one to three paragraphs, depending on the students. Leave the first and last sentence intact. For all remaining sentences, count to every fifth word, and put in a blank instead of the word. Students then read the selection and fill in all the blanks. It is one effective way to gauge a student's knowledge base.

Multiple-Choice Tests

Multiple-choice tests are probably the most used tests in classrooms across the nation. Their popularity is partly due to preparation for standardized tests and partly because they are easy to score. They also apply to a wide range of cognitive skills, including higher order thinking skills. Finally, incorrect answers, if written correctly, can help you diagnose a student's problem areas. Among their disadvantages are that the questions can't measure a student's ability to create or synthesize information and that students can guess at the correct answer.

One of the most important aspects of writing multiple-choice questions is creating the choices for the stem. If we are unclear, students can struggle. If we provide examples that are clearly off topic, it makes it easier for students to guess.

┌───┐
│
a. Avoid vague questions by stating the problem in the stem

Poor Example

California:

    a. Contains the tallest mountain in the United States.
    b. Has an eagle on its state flag.
│
└───┘

c. Is the second largest state in terms of area.

*d. Was the location of the Gold Rush of 1849.

Good Example

What is the main reason so many people moved to California in 1849?

a. California land was fertile, plentiful, and inexpensive.

*b. Gold was discovered in central California.

c. The east was preparing for a civil war.

d. They wanted to establish religious settlements.

b. Avoid implausible alternatives

Poor Example

Which of the following artists is known for painting the ceiling of the Sistine Chapel?

a. Warhol

b. Flintstone

*c. Michelangelo

d. Santa Claus

Good Example

Which of the following artists is known for painting the ceiling of the Sistine Chapel?

a. Botticelli

b. da Vinci

*c. Michelangelo

d. Raphael

Source: www.duq.edu/about/centers-and-institutes/center-for-teaching-excellence/teaching-and-learning/multiple-choice-exam-construction

Additionally, make the problem clear and avoid repeating parts of your question in the answer. It's also important to avoid clues to the response in your question. Finally, although some recommend excluding the choices "all of the above" and "none of the above," including those can increase the rigor because students have to make multiple decisions about the quality of responses.

> ### Tips for Writing Multiple-Choice Questions
>
> Keep reading level of question stem simple.
> Include a clear right or best answer.
> Keep all choices a similar length.
> Avoid grammatical cues (such as a plural word).
> Don't use *never* or *always*.
> Avoid negatives.
> Avoid patterns of correct answers (A, C, D, B, A, C, D, B).

Although many multiple-choice questions measure lower-level understanding, you can increase the rigor. For example, in her book *How to Design Questions and Tasks to Assess Student Thinking*, Susan Brookhart provides a comparison of two multiple-choice items, one that is more basic, and one that is at an increased level of rigor. In both, the student needs to know which character gives birth to twins, but notice the other information that must be understood in the second question.

Multiple-Choice Example 1
(Less Rigorous)

In E. B. White's essay "Twins," which character gives birth to twins?
  A. The speaker's mother
  B. A cow moose
  C. A red deer
  D. A shoe clerk

Multiple-Choice Example 2
(More Rigorous)

The following is from the first paragraph of the essay "Twins."
  They stood there, mother and child, under a gray beech whose trunk was engraved with dozens of hearts and initials.
  What does the sentence imply?
  A. E. B. White is sympathetic to parents and children.
  B. The deer were hiding from E. B. White and the other sightseers.
  C. E. B. White is aware of both nature and the urban setting.
  D. The graffiti interferes with E. B. White's enjoyment of the scene.

Short-Answer Questions

Short-answer questions are an expanded form of fill-in-the-blank questions. Responses are not as long as essays, but they usually include more than one sentence. Because students are required to create a response, they are more rigorous than the types of items we've already discussed. You'll need to build rigor into the context of your questions. Although they are more challenging to grade than matching, true-false, fill-in-the-blank, and multiple-choice questions, short-answer questions are simpler to assess than essay questions.

Less Rigorous Example

What are two ways in which the vast desert regions of Southwest and Central Asia affect the lives of the people who live there?

More Rigorous Example

Which desert, the Gobi or the Karakum, is easier to survive for those who might live there and why?

In order to write quality short-answer questions, be sure students know what they are expected to do. Keep the reading level low so that reading the question is not an obstacle to answering it. Finally, structure the question so that it requires a unique response.

Tips for Writing Short-Answer Questions

Avoid negative statements.
Keep writing spaces similar in length.
Keep the language of the question free of clues.
Ask direct questions.

One specific concern with both short-answer and essay questions is the vocabulary used in the questions. Earlier, we said to keep the reading level low, but what does that mean? First, avoid specialized vocabulary. In the prior example, it could be written as "Which desert, the Gobi or the Karakum, is more palatable for those who might live there and why?" But the word *palatable* is particularly challenging for students, so the question uses the phrase "easier to survive" instead. Additionally, for words such as *evaluate* and *analyze,* preteach the concepts prior to using them in a question.

Consider these recommendations for improving and increasing rigor of core assessments. What would you like to incorporate in your classroom or school?

The result of a benchmark assessment should be reviewed alongside the intervention progress monitoring graph to determine if any growth in the intervention may be related to growth in the core classroom. In other words, if growth is evident during intervention but there is little growth in the core, then the MTSS team must determine whether other changes must be made during core instruction or during intervention.

Data Review

Using the data from multiple sources, the MTSS team should review student data at least quarterly in order to more appropriately place, remove, or adjust students' intervention setting. However, many state departments and district teams recommend a frequent review. The reason for the frequent review is to use this data to predict students' next steps in an effort to maximize student learning. By examining progress monitoring data as well as other sources available, the team judges student performance to determine the most appropriate placement or adjustment within the current placement. If a student is not improving toward his or her goal, then different interventions and approaches should be made.

Intervention Analysis

Not only must school- and district-level MTSS teams review and choose interventions to match student needs, but they must also assess the effectiveness of the interventions. Most districts that we contacted conduct semi-annual to biannual reviews of not only their students but their intervention approaches and programs as well. Use the chart below to track the performance of students and the success of interventions.

Interventionist: _____	Progress Monitoring Trend Line Analysis				
Intervention: _____	August	September	October	November	December
Total number of students involved					
Number projecting toward goal					
Number performing parallel to goal line					
Number performing below goal line					

The time increments may be adapted based on when the MTSS team meets. Comparing the number of students who score at, above, or below the aim line shows how many students are progressing sufficiently using the intervention and how many are not. Over time and across several interventionists, an MTSS team can determine whether or not an intervention should be continued throughout a school or even a district. Further, it can help provide feedback to interventionists about their success in the intervention setting.

Potential Roadblocks With Progress Monitoring

When using progress monitoring, we provide a few cautions. The first is that many interventions programs also claim to act as a progress monitoring system. This shouldn't be the case. When progress monitoring and interventions are the exact same thing, it is likely that the only thing being done for the student is increased practice. Make sure that there are skills and strategies being taught in addition to a progress monitor.

The second is to be cautious of overreacting to progress monitoring data. After one week of an intervention, one would hope that the student would have a remarkable turnaround. However, that isn't likely, particularly for older students. Ask the interventionist and core teacher for input when reviewing data. The interventionist may provide valuable insight into the student's daily performance and even mindset. It may be that the student had other difficulties that required additional help. However, although we suggest that MTSS teams don't overreact to early data, we do suggest that they closely monitor progress so that they have an option to quickly move away from a potentially ineffective or misaligned intervention.

An additional caution is to make certain that assessments match each other in content. If a screener and progress monitor do not cover the same academic content, then results will appear varied. Additionally, if instruction content does not match the assessments, then determining progress will be misguided.

Conclusion

Assessment is a critical part of an MTSS program; it drives what occurs, from the placement to the instruction. It is important to choose appropriate assessments and to make sure that the assessments measure learning at a rigorous level.

7

Behavior and Social and Emotional Learning Through RTI/MTSS

An academic focus alone is not enough to improve the well-being of every student. Social emotional learning (SEL) is closely related to behavior and should be included as a part of an overall MTSS program. How can these also support rigor? Rigor includes having high expectations for students in all areas, not just academics. It also requires teachers to provide support so students can live up to those expectations.

Behavior

Behavior issues, from minor arguments and calling out in class to egregious offenses, occur in every school across the world. However, most behavior problems are usually handled in a reactive manner where reprimands follow actions deemed disruptive. Such reactions range from "the look" to verbal reprimands to lost free time to lost school time (i.e., suspensions). In many cases, these reactions serve as punishment because the student reduces the amount or intensity of the behavior. However, these reactions are sometimes ineffective or even escalate the inappropriate behavior. When inappropriate behaviors are repeated or become more common across a school, it is important to consider more positive approaches (Rodecki & Witzel, 2011).

A psychologically positive approach is not simply being happy; rather, it is being planful in your response to student behavior. A positive approach means that educators focus on what students are doing correctly or appropriately and praise those behaviors. By praising what is considered appropriate, the students learn what is expected of them. Otherwise, when students receive more feedback based on what they did inappropriately, attention is given to the wrong behavior, which may act as a reward for being disruptive.

Through a positive approach, reinforcement is connected to the behaviors that you want to see rather than what you don't want to see.

Positive Behavior Intervention Support

One approach that infuses a system of positive reinforcement is a Positive Behavior Intervention Support (PBIS), which includes a proactive plan to improve school climate and encourage appropriate behaviors for everyone. PBIS and MTSS are connected through a tiered approach and differentiation. When schools implement PBIS as part of core/tier 1 through tier 3 interventions, inappropriate and disruptive behavior decreases (Cheney et al., 2010; Sherrod, Getch, & Ziomek-Daigle, 2009).

Core Implementation

Michigan includes PBIS as part of its MTSS process and encourages it as a means of improving students' performance in school. As noted by Michigan's Integrated Learning and Behavior Support Initiative, PBIS means to create a welcoming and supportive school environment where appropriate behaviors are supported first and foremost. Appropriate behaviors are taught and even rewarded. By responding to students' acceptable behaviors during instruction, students receive feedback on what to expect of the classroom. In fact, in classes where the teacher focuses on students' appropriate behavior, engagement is much higher (Witzel, 2007).

A positive approach does not mean that inappropriate behaviors are ignored. Instead, inappropriate behaviors are handled through planned consequences and followed up by instruction and systematic rewards of acceptable behavior. For more information on the myths versus facts of PBIS, see https://miblsi.org/sites/default/files/Documents/MIBLSI_Sequence/District/DIT_Modules/SWPBISReadiness/03_SWPBIS_Myth_vs._Fact.pdf.

At the core level, we not only suggest initiating a PBIS approach, we recommend teaching rules to students as well as a creating a Bully Prevention system.

Establish and Teach Class Rules, Expectations, and Consequences

Students should be aware of what is expected of them as far as rules and consequences. Set up three to five positively stated rules so that students know what they should do rather than what they shouldn't do. Additionally, consequences should be clearly listed so that students know what will happen if they fail to comply with those rules.

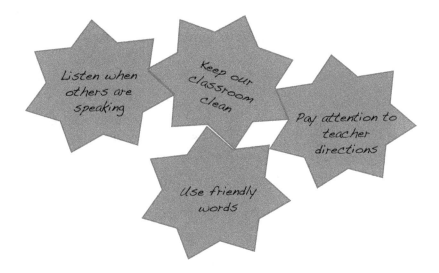

Once rules are established, it is important to teach the rules through direct instruction first (Conroy, Sutherland, Snyder, & Marsh, 2008), followed by role-play and activities (Rodecki & Witzel, 2011). Use examples of what each rule means and practice. Then, use one or two non-examples so that students understand when the rule doesn't apply. Consider showing videos of good behavior and even inappropriate behavior to initiate social interaction regarding behavior (Neitzel, 2010). Behavior games and scenarios can be effective ways to help prepare for more situations, increasing positive peer interactions and ultimately decreasing disruptive behavior.

Teach a School-Wide STOP Signal

The STOP signal, one method that is growing in popularity, is a quick verbal comment coupled with a simple physical signal that is agreed upon and taught to all students to use when they are being bullied or think someone else is being bullied. Teaching and supporting the STOP signal for both victims and bystanders has a history of success against school-based bullying. Using a system of STOP, Walk, and Talk (Ross, Horner, & Stiller, 2008), Nese and her colleagues found a decrease in verbal and physical aggression. The steps are as follows:

Teach How to Use the STOP Signal Through Both Examples and Non-Examples

When a student perceives an action as outside of what should be normal and potentially bullying, then that student and those around should use the STOP signal.

Examples of When to Use the STOP Signal	Non-Examples: When Not to Use the Signal
Adam calls Zehra a bad word. Billy trips Yasmin in the hallway. Callie repeatedly mocks Xavier on the bus ride home.	Wallace repeats his suggestion for a group project that Donna doesn't want to do. Vonda runs faster than Edgar in a game outside. Ulysses continues to tease Frank even after Frank said, "Stop."

If *stop* is not the chosen word, particularly for older students, then Ross and colleagues (2008) suggest replacing it with words like *enough* or *quit*.

Walk Away

Students should prepare for when the STOP signal does not stop the behavior. In such cases, teach the students to walk away. If the action against the student is truly bullying, then walking away removes the desired feedback for the bullying. Teach when to walk away for not only the potential victim but the bystanders as well. That way, the victim is supported.

Talk to an Adult

Show students how to tell an adult about the situation. Students should be prepared that the adult will ask if they said STOP and if they walked away. Differentiate tattling from talking to an adult. Ross and colleagues (2008) explain that tattling is when you didn't say STOP or walk away but went immediately to the adult without intervening in the situation. However, when students feel they are in danger, they should go quickly to seek adult help.

By infusing positive behavior management strategies into core class instruction, you will find that there are fewer disruptions and more time for active and engaged learning (Witzel, 2007). For more intense behavioral concerns, it is important to gather information through Functional Behavior Assessment protocol to determine the target behavior as well as the function of that inappropriate behavior. The focus of tiers 2 and 3 interventions should be on helping the students improve their behavior, keeping the function in mind.

> Has behavior been a challenge for you? Do these suggestions help? How will you incorporate them into your classroom or school?

Behavior and Tier 2

In tier 2 settings, take advantage of the smaller group sizes to increase interactions on behavior.

Mahad is repeatedly called names and even pushed by another student in the hallway between classes. What should Mahad do?

Such behavior scenarios can be used in a tier 2 setting as well, but the smaller group size will increase peer interactions, thus allowing and even making students openly reflect on the scenario. If reflection is too shallow, then consider starting a game: *Worst and Best Idea!* In this game, students work in pairs or even individually to develop the best idea to deal with a problem and the worst idea. The more varied the answers for both the worst and best, the better the conversation afterward about appropriate behavior, especially in tough situations.

Students in intervention settings should use a check-in/check-out system. In this system, the student starts every day with a school employee whom he or she trusts. This employee makes sure that the student has everything that he or she needs for the day. At the end of the brief meeting, the student is handed a progress report sheet. At the end of each class, the teacher checks off whether or not the student performed at an acceptable level and praises the student for what they did well. At the end of the day, the trusted employee debriefs with the student. Rewards or other consequences may be set to the results of the progress reports. The daily accountability and reinforcement helps keep the student engaged in school.

An additional strategy that works better in a small group is a token economy. Setting up a reward system that includes class money in exchange for such things as pencils, homework passes, paper, and extended free time is a way of increasing rewards for desired behavior. Such reinforcers are most effective when provided immediately following praise and a student's earning of a token. In a token economy, when a student expects a token but doesn't earn one, it is the teacher's responsibility to tell the student *why* they did not earn their token (Reitman, Murphy, Hupp, & O'Callaghan, 2004).

> Have you ever used tokens with your students? What worked? What didn't?

Behavior and Tier 3

There are several strategies that are designed for individual students. Although these can be delivered in core or tier 2 as well, we include them under tier 3 because of their individualized intention. MTSS models reserve tier 3 for the most severe behavior problems.

Self-Monitoring

When students do not respond well to group-level approaches, self-monitoring systems allow a student to track personal improvements toward reaching the desired behavioral response. To use a self-monitoring system, we suggest the following:

1. Help the student understand the desired behavior. This may be a replacement behavior to reduce the target behavior; for example, flipping a question card on the student's desk rather than calling out questions in class.
2. Place an index card on the student's desk and label what behavior is to occur. If appropriate, then list the replacement behavior. This allows the student to count the difference.

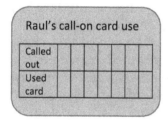
Raul's call-on card use

| Called out | | | | | | |
| Used card | | | | | | |

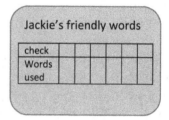
Jackie's friendly words

| check Words used | | | | | | |

3. Teach the student how to use the card.
4. Have the student check off the card during a designated time. This time should be when the target behavior occurs most frequently and a replacement behavior is needed the most.
5. Reflect with the student following the use of the card. Provide a reward as needed.
6. Graph results with the student to help the student see the changes over time. Praise and reward as needed.

Praise Notes

Praise notes are frequently written notes to a student that highlight the student's good behavior. In a tier 3 setting, praise notes can start as a pen pal–style note exchange system coupled with positive dialogue between teachers and students regarding behavior. This frequent interaction regarding the behavior allows the student to receive praise for appropriate behavior when simply reviewing the notes on his or her own. Although there has not been a great deal of research specifically on praise notes, it is a promising practice. Williamson and Witzel (2016) found qualitative signs of resilience in diverse students with and without disabilities in a case study using praise notes when the notes were written personally and reflected on student behavior.

Roadblocks to Behavior Intervention

Inconsistent Praise or Reinforcement Attempts

There are often concerns that some teachers will better adhere to a student's behavior plan than others. Help teachers by having biweekly discussions about fidelity of implementation. Also, reflect on class behavioral data to see differences that may indicate a lack of fidelity.

Behavior Gets Worse Before It Gets Better

Some students may not respond quickly to a behavior modification plan. Although this resistance is greater in reactive consequence plans, resistance may happen with positive plans as well. Most often, such stubborn resistance is related to more complex problems typically associated with extremely difficult behaviors and older students. Prepare all team members for this possibility, and remain vigilant in the implementation of a sound positive behavior plan. Revise the plan if a change does not occur after a few weeks.

Social Emotional Learning

SEL is closely related to issues of student behavior. The Collaborative for Academic, Social, and Emotional Learning describes SEL as the process of developing the following five sets of core competencies in the context of a safe, caring, well-managed, academically rigorous, and engaging classroom.

Core Competencies of SEL

- Self-awareness: Being able to accurately assess one's feelings, interests, values, and strengths; maintaining a well-grounded sense of self-confidence.
- Self-management: Being able to regulate one's emotions to handle stress, control impulses, and persevere in overcoming obstacles; setting and monitoring progress toward personal and academic goals; expressing emotions effectively.
- Social awareness: Being able to take the perspective of and empathize with others; recognizing and appreciating individual and

---

group similarities and differences; recognizing and using family, school, and community resources.

♦ Relationship skills: Being able to establish and maintain healthy and rewarding relationships based on cooperation; resisting inappropriate social pressure; preventing, managing, and resolving interpersonal conflict; seeking help when needed.

♦ Responsible decision-making: Being able to make decisions based on consideration of reason, ethical standards, safety concerns, social norms, respect for self and others, and likely consequences of various actions; applying decision-making skills to academic and social situations; contributing to the well-being of one's school.

Benefits of SEL

The pressures of standardized testing and accountability may make you wonder why you should take the time to teach social and emotional learning skills, especially because they are not tested. As with having a positive behavior system, teaching SEL typically results in fewer discipline problems, higher student engagement, and increased academic achievement. So, when we encourage positive social and emotional skills, we do impact student learning.

Strategies for Teaching SEL

Tom Roderick, executive director of Morningside Center for Teaching Social Responsibility and author of *A School of Our Own: Parents, Power, and Community at the East Harlem Block Schools*, describes several community-building activities to foster a culture of respect.

Sample SEL Activities

Name Games are a good way to start off the year. Kids stand in a circle and toss a soft ball to each other. When a student catches the ball, the class shouts out the student's name. The game continues till everyone gets a shout-out.

Have a Heart dramatizes the importance of making the classroom a "put-down-free zone." With a construction paper heart taped to her chest, the teacher tells the story of a student who experiences put-downs throughout her day. At each put-down, the teacher tears a piece from the heart. After a brief discussion ("Have you ever had a day like this? How do put-downs make us feel?"), she retells the story. But this time, the class substitutes put-ups for the put-downs.

Think Differently encourages students of all ages to engage in lively debate while acknowledging that we can disagree—and still treat each other with respect. The teacher tapes a "Strongly Agree" sign on one side of the classroom and a "Strongly Disagree" sign on the other. The teacher makes a statement, and students move to one sign or the other depending on whether they agree or disagree. If they're undecided, they stand in the middle. Statements can range from the trivial ("Vanilla ice cream is best") to the more serious ("Kids should only be allowed to watch one hour of TV per day" or "Slavery was the cause of the Civil War"). The teacher asks students in each group to explain their view, and students change position if they change their mind during the discussion. If the debate gets too heated, the teacher can ask students to paraphrase the opinion just expressed before putting out their own.

Source: http://novofoundation.org/newsfromthefield/several-ways-to-apply-social-emotional-learning-strategies-in-the-classroom/.

What strategies have you used to foster respect in your students? Is there one of these you might like to try?

Using Literature to Teach SEL

One way to teach social and emotional learning is to use literature. Children's books and young adult novels allow you to model effective SEL skills incorporated into your lessons.

Children's Books to Teach SEL

Abiyoyo by Pete Seeger.
Big Al by Andrew Clements.
Guess How Much I Love You by Sam McBratney.
I Can Share! by Karen Katz.
Mouse Was Mad by Linda Urban.
Quiet Loud by Leslie Patricelli.
No Biting! by Karen Katz.
"I Have a Problem," Said the Bear by Heinz Janischney.
Hands Are Not for Hitting by Martine Agassi.

Lesson plans for these books are available at http://csefel.vanderbilt.edu/resources/strategies.html.

There are also young adult novels that teach SEL, especially the value of hard work, good decision-making, and grit.

Young Adult Novels	
Sonia Nazario	*Enrique's Journey*
Pam Muñoz Ryan	*Esperanza Rising*
Gary Paulsen	*Hatchet*
Sharon Draper	*Out of My Mind*
Chris Crutcher	*Ironman*
Mildred D. Taylor	*Roll of Thunder, Hear My Cry*
Suzanne Collins	*The Hunger Games*
Timothée de Formbelle	*Toby and the Secrets of the Tree*
Lawrence Yep	*Dragonwings*

Mindful Practices SEL Framework

Carla Tantillo, author of *Everyday SEL* (2016), describes a mindful practices SEL framework.

Four Components of the Mindful Practices SEL Framework	
Component	*Aspects*
Self-awareness	Self-esteem, body awareness, personal responsibility, developing emotional awareness, and understanding choice.
Self-regulation	Adaptability, expressing emotions, managing stress and anxiety, problem solving, coping skills, and decision-making skills.
Social awareness	Active listening, empathy, service orientation, and community building.
Social regulation	Leadership, managing vulnerability, collaboration, teamwork, influence of self and others, relationship with self and others, and peer-to-peer communication.

Strategies for Teaching the Four Components

Tantillo (2016) also provides activities to meet each area of the framework.

Component	To begin, implement once or twice, three to five minutes a day, to shift frenetic student energy to calm, focused energy. Whole-class implementation is preferred with extended time for students with exceptionalities.
Self-awareness: Practicing these activities will help students move from powerlessness to self-control.	**Getting to Know My Emotions and Feelings:** Using stories, fables, photos, news articles, and real-life examples, introduce students to different emotions, such as sad, joyful, angry, frustrated, fearful, excited, and anxious, and/or different feelings, such as hungry, calm, focused, relaxed, tired, stressed, vulnerable, shameful, and hurt (physical vs. emotional). **Holding Who I Am:** Students trace their hand on a blank sheet of paper. Inside the hand, they write/draw all their strengths ("I am a good sibling," "I try my best in school," or "I am kind to others"). Around the outside of the hand, the students all write the challenges they are working on ("I will control my behavior during recess," "I will keep my eyes on my own paper during my spelling test," or "I will be kind to my little brother").
Self-regulation: Practicing these activities will help students move from impulsivity to navigating choices around their behavior.	**Cause & Effect Drawing:** Students record (write or draw) how x emotion or feeling prompts y action and how y action prompts z consequence (e.g., "When someone makes me angry, I swear/curse at them to get them back. When I use curse words in school, I get a detention"). **Write & Rip:** Students record (write or draw) negative feelings, experiences and emotions on a sheet of scrap paper. After writing for a set amount of time (four minutes on average), the students rip up their paper and toss it in the recycling bin, effectively letting go of negativity to help them be more centered and less reactive.

(Continued)

(Continued)

Social awareness: Practicing these activities will help students move from a reactive to a more communal view of the world.	**Memory Minute + Partner Reflection:** The teacher prompts a student to write a positive observation about his or her class on the board, such as "We are compassionate" or "We try our best." Students sit silently for one minute with their eyes closed, breathing and reflecting on the prompt and its connection to their classroom community. When the minute is up, the teacher calls on students to share one- or two-word examples of how the class exemplifies these qualities. The students' examples can be written on the board or recorded and hung on a poster in the room.
	Shoulder Share: Students sit shoulder to shoulder, facing opposite directions. The teacher gives the students a talking prompt, such as "How can we improve our behavior after lunch?" or "Preparing for the big test tomorrow." At the teacher's cue, one student shares his or her thoughts. The other student simply listens; he or she does not comment or critique his or her partner's thoughts. After a set amount of time (1.5 minutes on average), the students switch who is speaking and who is listening. When the activity concludes, the teacher may cue the students to share, depending on the topic.
Social regulation: Practicing these activities will help students move from feeling disconnected from the world around them to feeling like a valued and contributing member of their peer group.	**Service Learning Project:** Having students work collaboratively to create a service learning project is the perfect way to reinforce social regulation. Service learning projects are most successful when they bring different communities together, such as one classroom partnering with an older or younger grade to create a school green space or to put on a play at the local children's hospital.
	Compliment Circle: Students stand in two concentric circles facing each other, so that each student is standing across from a peer. The teacher prompts the students to share a time that the other student was exhibiting positive behavior, such as being kind, compassionate, caring, joyful, fun, or creative. Each student has one minute to share before the circle rotates

	to find new sets of partners. (For this to be successful, it is important for the teacher to appropriately frame the activity by discussing the difference between a true, observational compliment and a joke or self-deprecating comment.)

Does this information about SEL add to your understanding? If so, how?

Character Development

Several states have included laws to allow character education as part of their school curriculum. If a school or district chooses to implement a character education program, it is important to include input from not only educators but also community and parent leaders in order to address issues that may exist outside school. A character education program is designed to help students with not only SEL but also understanding of stewardship and social interactions. The Texas Education Code states that character education must include the following positive character traits:

a) courage;
b) trustworthiness (including honesty, reliability, punctuality, and loyalty);
c) integrity;
d) respect and courtesy;
e) responsibility (including accountability, diligence, perseverance, and self-control);
f) fairness (including justice and freedom from prejudice);
g) caring (including kindness, empathy, compassion, consideration, patience, generosity, and charity);
h) good citizenship (including patriotism, concern for the common good and the community, and respect for authority and the law); and
i) school pride.

(Texas Code § 29.906)

These traits are different from those in typical SEL programs. As such, a character education should be considered a part of rigorous expectations in teaching students to have high expectations of themselves both in and out of school. Comparing a sample character education program, Seven Mindsets (http://7mindsets.com), reveals an emphasis on improving yourself as well as those around you.

The Seven Mindsets

Everything Is Possible—Dream big, embrace creativity, and expect great results.

This first mindset involves setting one's goals high and planning to accomplish each goal.

Passion First—Pursue your authentic talents and deepest interests.

The second mindset helps students focus on their strengths rather than simply their weaknesses. This could be used to help hone the student's goals and see themselves as critically important to others. This will help build intrinsic motivation to overcoming likely obstacles in their path.

We Are Connected—Explore the synergies in all relationships and learn to empower one another.

This mindset teaches us to work with and rely on others to help us accomplish our goals. Everyone is unique in what they bring to us, so embracing diversity and internal competition can help us maximize our potential.

100% Accountable—Choose to be responsible for your own happiness and success.

By learning accountability, students are no longer victims of their pasts but rather can take critical steps toward accomplishing their goals.

Attitude of Gratitude—Seek positives from every experience and be thankful for all you have.

This mindset teaches students to make decisions that will positively impact their lives.

Live to Give—Inspire and serve others while maximizing your potential.

In order to receive, we must first learn to give. Students learn to affect the world around them so that it, in return, positively affects them.

The Time Is Now—Harness the power of this moment, and take purposeful action today.

The final mindset is to create a sense of urgency in making change to help students set their plans and actions in motion.

We suggest that schools consider adopting a whole-school approach that brings positive behavior support and frequent dialogue on behavior and SEL. Including the school, parents, and the community in the decision only strengthens the connection between the school and the surrounding community.

Conclusion

Many teachers find themselves struggling to maintain control of their classroom when using reactive discipline practices. Although it may take many years for schools to fully implement a PBIS system (Bradshaw, Reinke, Brown, Bevans, & Leaf, 2008), teachers can still integrate the principles behind those programs into their daily classroom management and discipline routines. By implementing PBIS strategies, teachers can spend more time teaching and less time writing discipline referrals. Additionally, focusing on SEL is worthwhile. SEL helps students grow behaviorally, which ultimately results in increased learning at rigorous levels.

8

Working Together
The RTI/MTSS Leadership Team

Leadership makes or breaks a system, whether that system is a school, a business, a home, or an MTSS program. Forming and developing MTSS leadership teams at the building and district levels is important for many reasons. The leadership team sets up and leads the MTSS meetings, reviews data, makes instructional and curricular decisions (in part to ensure rigor), targets professional development opportunities matched to teacher and student needs, coaches and supports teachers and interventionists, monitors and adjusts assessment schedules, and ensures fidelity throughout.

Sharing a Vision

The first step in building an effective team is to create a vision. Theodore Hesburgh noted, "The very essence of leadership is [that] you have a vision. It's got to be a vision you articulate clearly and forcefully on every occasion. You can't blow an uncertain trumpet." Too often, we jump into the logistics of managing the team and the MTSS program, and there is not a shared vision. One activity Barbara and Ron Williamson (2017) recommended you complete with your group is Hot Air Balloon.

Hot Air Balloon Vision Activity

Ask each person on the team to list their ideas individually, then share them with the group. Finally, collaborate to create a shared list that everyone can support. Do this for each step.

Step 1

Imagine you are in a hot air balloon high in the sky over our school.
You are looking down at our MTSS program.
What do you see? What can you hear?

---

*It is five years from now, and you have returned in your hot air balloon.
Things have changed, and it is now the most effective MTSS program
in our state.
What do you see? What do you hear?*

Once you have completed both steps, compare the shared lists.
Ask participants to identify what they want to change or improve to
reach their ideal vision.

Now that you have a shared vision and a clear idea of what you want
to accomplish, it's time to move on to the structure of leading the MTSS
program.

Oregon Response to Intervention and Instruction (2016) highlighted the
numerous benefits of MTSS, including increased collaboration:

Many benefits [of MTSS] have been reported by the districts that
we serve . . . improved instructional practices, increased collaboration among staff, a greater cohesion of instructional service delivery,
enhanced efficiency of service delivery, and improved outcomes for
students are some of the key things that staff report.

Importance of Collaboration

The effectiveness of your MTSS program will be enhanced if you have
teachers and leaders working together. Isolated attempts to meet students'
needs simply do not work in the MTSS program.

Benefits and Challenges of Collaboration and Shared Decision-Making

Collaboration is the most critical aspect of an effective MTSS team. There
are many benefits, but there are also some challenges.

Benefits	*Challenges*
◆ Higher-quality decisions because more perspectives are considered.	◆ Expanded participation may require more time to make decisions.

◆ Increased job satisfaction and morale. ◆ Heightened sense of empowerment. ◆ Greater ownership of goals and priorities when participants have a stake in the decision. ◆ Improved student achievement because of greater coordination of work among stakeholders.	◆ Group dynamics may stifle ideas, leading to "groupthink". ◆ Polarization around specific points of view. ◆ People feeling left out or that some have greater access and opportunity to influence decisions.

Overall, the long-term benefits of shared decision-making outweigh the initial, mostly short-term obstacles. When employees are active partners in critical decisions about the MTSS program, they have more ownership of the program's direction and a greater commitment to its success.

Does your team collaborate effectively? Are there areas of improvement?

Who Should Be on the MTSS Team?

A broad range of people are involved in an effective MTSS program. Each has a particular role in the process.

Person/Job Title	Main Responsibilities
Core Teachers	Provide core instruction for all students.
Special Education Teacher	Assist team with accommodations and differentiation.
Gifted Education Teacher	Assist team with differentiation and gifted intervention and acceleration.
Grade/Course Team Leader	Instructional direction.
Interventionists	Provide tier 2 and 3 interventions; collaborate with core teacher.

Behavioral Specialist/ Counselor	Leads behavioral decisions.
School Psychologist	Assessment leadership.
School Administrators	MTSS leadership.
District Math Director	Math curriculum selection and adjustments.
District Reading/Literacy Director	Literacy curriculum selection and adjustments.
Other District Administrators	District-level MTSS leadership.

Most of these roles are self-explanatory, but we want to take a moment to address one group specifically: that of the interventionist.

Interventionists

Select interventionists based on their knowledge of instructional strategies and the construct that is the focus of the intervention. In other words, if a tier 2 intervention is needed for letter sounds, then a teacher trained in early literacy intervention is a prime choice. It is important to make sure that the training is focused on intervention delivery rather than generic or less intensive strategies. Tier 3 intervention delivery requires even more intense trainings for the interventionist. Do not let the small group size or even a one-to-one setting fool you into thinking that anyone with minimal training will succeed. Tier 3 intervention requires deeper content and intervention knowledge. Instructional coaches and special education teachers are often lead candidates for tier 3 intervention because of their familiarity and training with specialized, intensive interventions. Although special educators may be more familiar with conducting and assessing intensive interventions, it is important to check that the content knowledge of the interventionist and their understanding of the academic construct is appropriate.

Application of Tier 1 Roles and Responsibilities

To increase teacher involvement in the decision-making process and the training needed to improve instruction and intervention delivery, Oregon Response to Intervention and Instruction (2016) suggested setting up tier 1 focused professional learning communities with grade-level and course-level teachers to review, share, and enact targeted instructional strategies, such as explicit instruction or culturally responsive teaching, as it relates to the data-based need. Along with tier 1 teachers, involve the interventionist on more than intervention trainings so that a clear dialogue will strengthen the communication between core instruction and interventionists.

Co-Teaching in the Core Classroom

One question that core teachers often ask is "How do I work with teachers of students with special needs?" Marilyn Friend and Lynn Cook (2016) described six models of co-teaching.

Models of Co-Teaching

1. **One Teach, One Observe:** One of the advantages in co-teaching is that more detailed observation of students engaged in the learning process can occur. With this approach, for example, co-teachers can decide in advance what types of specific observational information to gather during instruction and can agree on a system for gathering the data. Afterward, the teachers should analyze the information together.
2. **One Teach, One Assist:** One person keeps primary responsibility for teaching while the other circulates through the room, providing unobtrusive assistance to students as needed.
3. **Parallel Teaching:** The teachers are both covering the same information, but they divide the class into two groups and teach simultaneously.
4. **Station Teaching:** Teachers divide content and students. Each teacher then teaches the content to one group and subsequently repeats the instruction for the other group.
5. **Alternative Teaching:** One teacher takes responsibility for the large group while the other works with a smaller group.
6. **Team Teaching:** Both teachers are delivering the same instruction at the same time. This approach is sometimes called tag team teaching.

There is not a perfect model; the one used should match students' needs. Teachers should work together to determine how to teach together, and that may vary with different lessons. The only guideline is this: neither teacher should be treated as "less than" the other.

In your core classrooms, what model do you use? Is there one from the list above you would like to try?

Role of Personnel Within the Overall MTSS Program

Matching roles and responsibilities to MTSS leaders in a school and district is important for the overall success of the program. In the sample assignment list below, each member is a contributing member at MTSS meetings but the leader of the specific components of MTSS and key personnel who should be consulted on important decisions are highlighted. Each person assigned a Leader (L) or Facilitator (F) role should have training for that component.

Sample MTSS Assignment List												
MTSS Component L = Leader F = Facilitator	Due Date	District Administrators	School Administrators	School Psychologist	District Reading/Literacy Director	District Math Director	Grade/Course Team Leader	Interventionists	Core Teachers	Special Education Teacher	Gifted Education Teacher	Behavioral Specialist/Counselor
Sets Assessment Schedule	May	L	F	F								
Sets MTSS Meeting Schedule	May		L	F								
Reviews Student Scores for Placement	Quarterly		F	L				F				
Makes Core Curriculum Decisions	Annually				L	L	F		F			
Makes Core Instruction Recommendations	Semiannually				F	F	L	F	F			
Makes Intervention Program Decisions	Annually				L	L		F				

Makes Intervention Recommendations	Quarterly			F	F			L			
Decides Special Education Placement	Per Placement Meeting	F		F					L		
Makes Behavioral Recommendations	Per Placement Meeting			F				F	F		L
Makes Gifted Recommendations	Semiannually		F	F			F			L	
Coaches and Supports Teachers	Ongoing		F			F	F	L			F
Targets Professional Development Opportunities	Annually	L	F			F	F	F			F
Implements Core Instruction and Adaptations	Ongoing					F	F	L	F	F	F
Implements Interventions	Ongoing					F	L	F	F	F	F

Source: Adapted from the work presented by Ted and Jennifer Gennerman (2016).

Leaders and Facilitators

Although the Leader and Support roles listed in the example may match your scenario and local expertise, for others it may not. It is important to assign leaders who understand their tasks and can hold others accountable. Additionally, leaders may not have such titles designated in their job description, but they have the ability to lead and the knowledge to be effective. In those cases, it is even more important for school- and district-level administrators to support the leader. An important consideration when assigning roles is the difference between special and general education certification. As several of the states and districts who helped us with this book reminded us, MTSS is *not* special education. Despite high involvement from special education as well as numerous lawsuits surrounding child find and special education placement (Moore, Sabousky, & Witzel, 2017), the purpose of MTSS is to improve outcomes for all students. Placing too much leadership in the hands of special educators leaves other stakeholders to believe that this is a special education initiative that only affects eligibility and students with potential disabilities.

Professional Development and Training

It is important to involve teachers throughout the MTSS process, whether they take over a leadership role or a support role in intervention placement, curriculum and instructional decisions, or the data review process. Although participation is important for developing buy-in, when initiating a comprehensive school reform project, it is even more important to infuse the following:

♦ Training for instruction and intervention delivery.
♦ Curriculum support.
♦ Teacher say over core implementation.
♦ Administrator buy-in.

(Turnbull, 2002)

Sustained training for each member of the team helps support evidence-supported practices and validates the hard work from the team. As we shared in Chapter 2, based on research with schools that have won the U.S. Department of Education's Award for Staff Learning (Blackburn, 2000), there are seven key elements of effective professional learning. Each should be considered when providing training.

Key Elements of Effective Professional Learning

1. Clear purpose linked to research, student data, goals, and needs.
2. Accountability through classroom use of ideas and impact on students.
3. Learning of a common, shared language.
4. Shared decision-making, which includes an emphasis on teacher input.
5. Incorporation of relevant, practical, hands-on activities.
6. Integration of opportunities for follow-up and application.
7. Strong leadership and a positive, collegial atmosphere.

What professional development has occurred in your school? Is there additional professional development needed? If so, how will you plan it based on the characteristics of effective professional development?

Next, curriculum support and teacher involvement in core implementation are important because, as stated repeatedly in this book, the foundation of a strong MTSS approach is an effective tier 1 approach. Throughout all planning, keep core instruction in mind as a foundation. Finally, without the support of both district and school administration, the effectiveness of MTSS will be minimal. Years of research from the Wallace Foundation (2011) has found that school leadership is empirically linked to student achievement.

An MTSS Problem-Solving Approach

After identifying who is struggling or at risk of struggling academically, it is important to determine how best to help the student. MTSS placement meetings should be held a minimum of four times of year. However, we recommend more frequent meetings in order to check student progress and make reactive decisions based on that data. By having monthly or semi-quarterly meetings, teams are able to make adjustments to a student's intervention in order to maximize their growth toward their goal. Such meetings also allow for conversations on instructional delivery at all levels.

Conducting Effective Meetings

Meetings are an important part of a successful MTSS program. However, we have all attended meetings that were unproductive and frustrating. A crucial part of any effective meeting is having a set of meeting standards or operational norms. This includes basic decisions such as the seating arrangements. If you want an open discussion, try to arrange for participants to face each other, perhaps around a table or in a semicircle rather than in rows. Set a firm start and end time, and stick to them. This shows that you respect the participants' time. If the meeting is lengthy, plan for a break, but again, set a time for it and adhere to that. Be sure that any speaker knows his or her allocated time and stays within those parameters.

Ask yourself, "How will we maintain our group memory of discussion and decisions?" Do you want to use charts posted visibly in the room, or will you have someone record notes? How can you utilize the technological equipment you have to support the process? You might even consider recording the meeting. A public recording provides visual clues, develops shared ownership, minimizes repetition, reduces status differences among participants, and makes accountability easier.

What are the guidelines for discussion? We often use a "parking lot," which is simply a poster in the room. Participants are given sticky notes, and if they have a question or discussion item that is off topic, they write it on a note and post it in the parking lot. You can revisit those items at the end of the meeting if there is time, or you can discuss them individually or at another time.

It's also important to model collaborative discussion. Allowing adequate wait time in response to questions, asking open-ended questions, and giving everyone a chance to speak are the foundational elements of a collaborative discussion. Garmston and Wellman (2013) describe seven norms of collaboration that are helpful.

Seven Norms of Collaboration

Pausing: Pausing before responding or asking a question allows time for thinking and enhances dialogue, discussion, and decision-making.

Paraphrasing: Using a paraphrase starter that is comfortable for you, such as "As you are . . ." or "You're thinking . . .," and following the starter with a paraphrase assists members of the group to hear and understand each other as they formulate decisions.

Probing: Using gentle open-ended probes or inquiries such as, "Please say more . . ." or "I'm curious about . . ." or "I'd like to hear more about . . ." or "Then, are you saying . . .?" increases the clarity and precision of the group's thinking.

Putting Ideas on the Table: Ideas are the heart of a meaningful dialogue. Label the intention of your comments. For example, you might say, "Here is one idea . . ." or "One thought I have is . . ." or "Here is a possible approach . . ."

Paying Attention to Self and Others: Meaningful dialogue is facilitated when each group member is conscious of self and of others and is aware of not only what he or she is saying but also how it is said and how others are responding. This includes paying attention to learning style when planning for, facilitating, and participating in group meetings.

Presuming Positive Intentions: Assuming that others' intentions are positive promotes and facilitates meaningful dialogue and eliminates unintentional put-downs. Using positive intentions in your speech is one manifestation of this norm.

Pursuing a Balance Between Advocacy and Inquiry: Pursuing and maintaining a balance between advocating a position and inquiring about one's own and others' positions assists the group to become a learning organization.

Source: Garmston & Wellman (2013).

Making Decisions: PAIR Instructional Model

Little (2013) supported the PAIR Instructional Decision-Making model when reviewing student data for an intervention placement or movement decision:

Problem Identification—Screening data is used to determine the general area(s) in which a student is struggling. Screeners give a general overview of how students are performing on a normed scale, either locally or nationally.

Analysis of the Problem—Determine why the student is struggling. Students should be identified to diagnostics and error pattern analysis. As stated in Chapter 6, either the school should have a diagnostic assessment completed on each student of concern or the core teachers should be notified so that they may conduct a formative diagnostic inventory of the student's performance.

Intervention Design and Implementation—Based on the information from the diagnostic, determine the level of intervention support that is needed. Ask: Could this be addressed effectively in the tier 1 setting by the core teacher? Or does the student require intervention? If so, at what level? Once the level of intensity is decided, then the difficulty of scheduling must be addressed. If something as seemingly minor as fractions is identified as a significant weakness in a middle school student and the team determines that a tier 2 intervention is sufficient, then the team must work with the interventionist to determine how best to address that need in tier 2. How many other students require this need? How quickly can we begin? When might this intervention best be delivered? Once decided, then the goal is set for the student and an implementation strategy is designed.

Respond to the Data—Within the first couple of weeks, data should be reviewed to determine if the intervention is having a positive effect and if the rate of improvement is sufficient to meet the goal by the designated time. If not, why not? If not, then what changes are needed? Additionally, progress in the core should be assessed to make sure that the intervention content is adequately improving the student's performance in the core classroom. If not, why not? If not, then what changes are needed? This open dialogue requires frequent communication among the team, particularly the core classroom teacher and the interventionist.

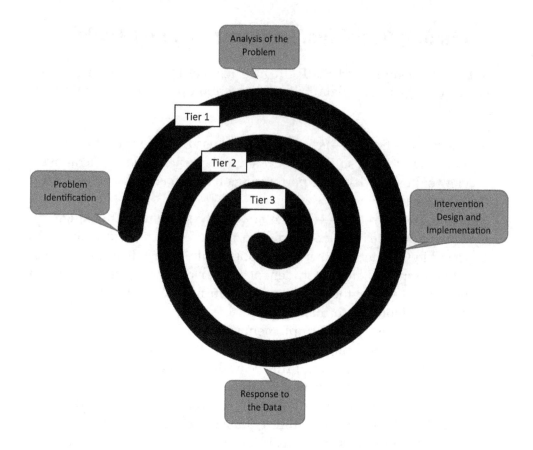

Alternative Problem-Solving Model

Most states support a problem-solving decision model similar to PAIR. For example, the Colorado Department of Education advocates a problem-solving model where MTSS teams review and respond to student data through a Define, Analyze, Implement, Evaluate approach (www.cde. state.co.us/mtss/problemsolvingprocesspages). Colorado also encourages monthly data collection and discussion to support this model.

Colorado Suggested Meeting Agenda

1. Review notes and data from previous meetings.
   a. Review notes from the previous meeting.
   b. Review previous intervention plans and supports.
   c. Review previous data for each student.
2. Set the objectives for each student.
   a. Follow the PAIR problem-solving approach.
   b. Compare most frequent assessment data with previous data.
   c. Make predictions about the student's performance.

---

3. Assign tasks.
   a. Assign roles for implementation, collaboration, and review.
   b. Set a timeline for the next review.

Hoover (2010) recommended that during each meeting, teams should include conversations on research-supported approaches as well as the fidelity of instruction and assessment implementation. The purpose is not only to improve the delivery and effectiveness of the approach, but in the case that this leads to special education identification, it is also important to know that each step was addressed as accurately and appropriately as possible. Instructional fidelity is a concern when it comes to implementation and analysis. When teachers agree on implementation of a program or intervention, then data may be analyzed uniformly. However, when a teacher decides to vary from the agreed-upon approach and infuse what wasn't considered a best practice in the team meeting, then that data, whether superior or inferior to others' data, invalidates any analysis of the program or approach.

For example, if a second-grade teacher and interventionist agree on a reading comprehension strategy, then that same strategy should be used consistently and equally in both settings. If it is not, then the student will likely get confused as to the strategy and the data will not support the use of that strategy. By undermining the agreed-upon approach, the student suffers and the future use of an effective strategy may also suffer because the data will reveal that the strategy was not effective for that student. Therefore, we recommend that coaches and administrators review the implementation of strategies, programs, and assessment delivery for fidelity. When in doubt, those involved should be brought together to practice what is weak in fidelity until all parties can deliver the approach equally.

How would the PAIR model help you and others in your school and district improve your efforts?

Results: Intervene Quickly to Meet Students' Needs Based on Data

Although we have advocated for patience with interventions in previous chapters, we don't want this patience to be misconstrued as not providing tiered intervention when students need support. Waiting for appropriate interventions to be delivered can have deleterious effects on student achievement. In an early literacy study, Al Otaiba and her team (2014) found that when MTSS teams delayed intervention asking for tier 1 support only, the students scored significantly lower in their reading. Conversely, those who received interventions soon after screening measures were reviewed also received immediate reading score effects, and those effects continued across the academic year. Thus, it is important to be quickly reactive to student scores when deciding student interventions.

Beginning a School-Wide or District-Wide Implementation

At its core, MTSS should help all students improve performance (Burns & Van Der Hayden, 2006). As such, implementing an MTSS model should develop in a stepwise fashion that increases buy-in and touches every student, whether receiving tiered intervention, gifted acceleration, or simply high-quality core instruction. The following is a three-year rollout plan for establishing MTSS in a school. To get started, use this chart to see what needs to happen at your school along the path of full implementation. Add to it or subtract from it based on the needs of your students. If your school has already started this process, use this chart to patch holes or plan next steps. There is no one way to roll out MTSS (www.rtinetwork.org/getstarted/implement/implementyourplan) or any reform movement, for that matter, so it is wise to make long-term goals and keep everyone informed about the next steps along the way. If MTSS is viewed as just another reform project, then even some of the leaders will be waiting for it to fade away. If, however, a long-term implementation chart is displayed and tracked, then everyone involved will see what is happening, what will happen, and what their role will be in the future.

Three-Year Rollout Plan	Summer Before Year 1: Planning	Year 1 Core: Identify Needs	Year 2: Initiating Intervention	Year 3: Full System of Support
Assessment				
Universal Screener	Select	Implement 2x/year minimum	Implement 2x/year minimum	Implement 2x/year minimum
Benchmark/Progress Monitor	Develop standards-based benchmark/PM assessment	Implement 4x/year minimum	Implement 4x/year minimum	Implement 8x/year minimum
Diagnostic	Select diagnostic approach	Implement diagnostic at core level during key standards	Implement during core and intervention	Implement during core and intervention
Data Team				
Role Selection	Select data team leaders	Select data team and train	Review and revise approach	Review and revise approach

(continued)

Review Schedule	Set four data days/year minimum	Review screener and PM	Review screener and PM	Consider eight data days/year; review screener and PM
Intervention Selection		Select deficit areas across grades and content	Revise core and intervention content	Revise core and intervention content
Core Suggestions	Make suggestions for training	Make differentiation suggestions based on screener; implement PD	Differentiation and core intervention delivery; follow-up PD	Differentiation and core intervention delivery follow-up PD
Tier 1 Instruction Delivery				
Establish Instructional Nonnegotiables	Data team decides on core nonnegotiables	Display nonnegotiables	Revise nonnegotiables	Revise nonnegotiables
Professional Development		Core PD on nonnegotiables	Core and interventionist PD on nonnegotiables	Core and interventionist PD on nonnegotiables

Fidelity Review		Develop teacher teams and peer review	Data team and peer reviews	Data team and peer reviews
Intervention Delivery				
Schedule		Schedule intervention times	Implement intervention times	Revise intervention times
Set Collaboration Connections		Data team and core teachers	Core and interventionists with data team	Core and interventionists with data team
Review Core Performance	Review all data available	Review end-of-year data	Review end-of-year data	Review end-of-year data

Source: This chart was adapted based on work from the rtinetwork.org and the Central New York Regional Implementation Center: www.cnyric.org/tfiles/folder973/Generic%20RTI%20Implementation%20Timetable%20Resource.pdf

Conclusion

The MTSS team is the most important aspect of improving student performance using this model. Decide who should be involved and what each person's responsibility will be. Bring the team together before enacting MTSS so that everyone understands his or her role and how important it is to collaborate with one another. Set and maintain the mission of your MTSS team as a means to positively impact every student's achievement and to ensure a high level of rigor for each student. Prepare for the potential pitfalls and prepare how to tackle them. When an easy solution isn't available, bring the issue to a faculty meeting so that everyone can help address it. Help everyone in a school recognize that every student is every teacher's responsibility.

Once you have established your tiered system and your MTSS team understands their roles, it is time to pilot the process. Believe in your students and your teachers' instruction. Show the confidence you would have when reading a suspense novel after you've already read the last chapter. You know what will happen, and you know the improvements that will be made. Celebrate the efforts and resulting strides that teachers make, and congratulate students for their improvements. Be assured, however, that the result will be based on your planning and ongoing work to ensure student success.

Bibliography

ACT. (2006). *Reading between the lines: What the ACT reveals about college readiness in reading*. Iowa City, IA: ACT.

ACT. (2011). *The condition of college and career readiness*. Iowa City, Iowa: Experiment examining first-grade response to intervention in reading. *Exceptional Children, 81*(1), 11–27.

Al Otaiba, S., Wagner, R. K., & Miller, B. (2014). "Waiting to fail" redux: Understanding inadequate response to intervention. *Learning Disability Quarterly, 37*(3), 129–133.

Allen, Janet. (2007). *Inside words: Tools for teaching academic vocabulary. Grades 4–12*. Portland, Maine: Stenhouse Publishers.

Anderson, L. W. (Ed.), Krathwohl, D. R. (Ed.), Airasian, P. W., Cruikshank, K. A., Mayer, R. E., Pintrich, P. R., Raths, J., & Wittrock, M. C. (2001). *A taxonomy for learning, teaching, and assessing: A revision of Bloom's Taxonomy of educational objectives*. New York: Longman.

Archer, A. L., & Hughes, C. A. (2011). *Explicit instruction: Effective and efficient teaching*. New York: Guilford Press.

Armstrong, A., Ming, K., & Helf, S. (in press). Content area literacy in the mathematics classroom. *Clearing House*.

Ausubel, D. P., Novak, J. D., & Hanesian, H. (1978). *Educational psychology: A cognitive view* (2nd ed.). New York: Holt, Rinehart, and Winston.

Blackburn, B. R. (2000). *Barriers and facilitators of effective staff development: Perceptions from award-winning practitioners*. Unpublished doctoral dissertation, University of North Carolina at Greensboro.

Blackburn, B. R. (2008). *Literacy from A to Z: Engaging students in reading, writing, speaking, and listening*. New York: Routledge.

Blackburn, B. R. (2012). *Rigor is not a four-letter word* (1st ed). New York: Routledge.

Blackburn, B. R. (2012a). *Rigor made easy*. New York: Routledge.

Blackburn, B. R. (2012b). *Rigor is not a four-letter word* (2nd ed.). New York: Routledge.

Blackburn, B. R. (2014). *Rigor in your classroom: A toolkit for teachers*. New York: Routledge.

Blackburn, B. R. (2016a). *Classroom instruction from A to Z: How to promote student learning* (2nd ed.). New York: Routledge.

Blackburn, B. R. (2016b). *Motivating struggling learners: Ten strategies for student success*. New York: Routledge.

Blackburn, B. R. (2017). *Rigor and assessment in the classroom*. New York: Routledge.

Blackburn, B. R. (2018). *Rigor is* not *a four-letter word* (3rd ed.). New York: Routledge.

Blackburn, B. R., & Witzel, B. (2013). *Rigor for students with special needs.* New York: Routledge.

Boon, R. T., & Spencer, V. G. (2013). *Adolescent literacy strategies for content comprehension in inclusive classrooms.* Baltimore, MD: Paul H. Brookes.

Bottoms, G., & Timberlake, A. (2008). *Preparing middle grades students for high school success.* Atlanta, GA: Southern Regional Education Board.

Bradshaw, C. P., Reinke, W. M., Brown, L. D., Bevans, K. B., & Leaf, P. J. (2008). Implementation of school-wide positive behavioral interventions and supports (PBIS) in elementary schools: Observations from a randomized trial. *Education & Treatment of Children, 31*(1), 1–26.

Brookhart, S. (2014). *How to design questions and tasks to assess student thinking.* Alexandria, VA: ASCD.

Bryant, D. P., Bryant, B. R., Gersten, R., Scammacca, N., & Chavez, M. (2008). Mathematics intervention for first and second grade students with mathematics difficulties: The effects of Tier 2 intervention delivered as booster lessons. *Remedial and Special Education, 29*(1), 20–32.

Bryant, D. P., Ugel, N., Thompson, S., & Hamff, A. (1999). Instructional strategies for content-area reading instruction. *Intervention in School and Clinic, 34*(5), 293–302.

Burns, M. K., & Van Der Hayden, A. M. (2006). Using response to intervention to assess learning disabilities: Introduction to the special series. *Assessment for Effective Intervention, 32,* 3–5.

Chapman, C. M., & King, R. S. (2012). *Differentiated assessment strategies.* Thousand Oaks, CA: Corwin.

Chapman, C. M., & Vagle, N. (2011). *Motivating students: 25 strategies to light the fire of engagement.* Bloomington, IN: Solution Tree.

Cheney, D., Lynass, L., Flower, A., Waugh, M., Iwaszuk, W., Mielenz, C., & Hawken, L. (2010). The check, connect, and expect program: A targeted, Tier 2 intervention in the schoolwide positive behavior support model. *Preventing School Failure, 54*(3), 152–158.

Conroy, M. A., Sutherland, K. S., Snyder, A. L., & Marsh, S. (2008). Classwide interventions. *Teaching Exceptional Children, 40*(6), 24–30.

Cortiella, C., & Horowitz, S. H. (2014). *The state of learning disabilities* (3rd ed.). New York: National Center for Learning Disabilities. Retrieved from www.ncld.org/wp-content/uploads/2014/11/2014-State-of-LD.pdf

Darling-Hammond, L., & Adamson, F. (2014). *Beyond the Bubble Test: How Performance Assessments Support 21st Century Learning.* Jossey-Bass/Wiley.

Doren, B., Murray, C., & Gau, J. M. (2014). Salient predictors of school dropout among secondary students with learning disabilities. *Learning Disabilities Research & Practice, 29*(4), 150–159.

Dorman, C., Wheeler, D., & Diamond, H. (2010). *Problem solving and response to intervention*. Florida Department of Education. Retrieved from www.fldoe.org/core/fileparse.php/3/urlt/psrti.rtf

Epstein, M., Atkins, M., Cullinan, D., Kutash, K., & Weaver, R. (2008). *Reducing behavior problems in the elementary school classroom: A practice guide* (NCEE 2008–012). Washington, DC: National Center for Education Evaluation and Regional Assistance, Institute of Education Sciences, U.S. Department of Education.

Foorman, B., Beyler, N., Borradaile, K., Coyne, M., Denton, C. A., Dimino, J., . . . Wissel, S. (2016). *Foundational skills to support reading for understanding in kindergarten through 3rd grade* (NCEE 2016–4008). Washington, DC: National Center for Education Evaluation and Regional Assistance (NCEE), Institute of Education Sciences, U.S. Department of Education.

Forehand, M. (2005). Bloom's taxonomy: Original and revised. In M. Orey (Ed.), *Emerging perspectives on learning, teaching, and technology*. Retrieved April 22, 2017, from http://epltt.coe.uga.edu/

Friend, M., & Cook, L. (2016). *Interactions: Collaboration skills for school professionals* (8th ed.). Boston: Pearson.

Frye, D., Baroody, A. J., Burchinal, M., Carver, S. M., Jordan, N. C., & McDowell, J. (2013). *Teaching math to young children: A practice guide* (NCEE 2014–4005). Washington, DC: National Center for Education Evaluation and Regional Assistance (NCEE), Institute of Education Sciences, U.S. Department of Education.

Fuchs, D., Fuchs, L., Mathes, P., & Martinez, E. (2002). Preliminary evidence on the social standing of students with learning disabilities in PALS and no-PALS classrooms. *Learning Disability Research and Practice*, 17(4), 205–215. Retrieved from http://eds.a.ebscohost.com.winthropuniversity.idm.oclc.org/ehost

Garmston & Wellman. (2013). *Seven norms of collaboration*. Retrieved from www.thinkingcollaborative.com/norms-collaboration-toolkit/

Gennerman, T., & Gennerman, J. (2016, August 26). Written and personal interview with Dr. Brad Witzel.

Gersten, R., Beckmann, S., Clarke, B., Foegen, A., Marsh, L., Star, J. R., & Witzel, B. (2009). *Assisting students struggling with mathematics: Response to Intervention (RTI) for elementary and middle schools* (NCEE 2009–4060). Washington, DC: National Center for Education Evaluation and Regional Assistance, Institute of Education Sciences, U.S. Department of Education.

Gersten, R., Compton, D., Connor, C. M., Dimino, J., Santoro, L., Linan-Thompson, S., & Tilly, W. D. (2008). *Assisting students struggling with reading: Response to Intervention and multi-tier intervention for reading in the primary grades: A practice guide* (NCEE 2009–4045). Washington, DC: National Center for Education Evaluation and Regional Assistance, Institute of Education Sciences, U.S. Department of Education.

Graham, S., & Hebert, M. A. (2010). *Writing to read: Evidence for how writing can improve reading: A Carnegie Corporation Time to Act report*. Washington, DC: Alliance for Excellent Education.

Hattie, J. (2008). *Visible learning: A synthesis of over 800 meta-analyses relating to achievement*. New York: Routledge.

Hattie, J. (2012).*Visible learning for teachers: Maximizing impact on learning*. New York: Routledge.

Hattie, J., Masters, D., Birch, K. (2015). *Visible learning into action: International case studies of impact*. New York: Routledge.

Heller, J. I., Daehler, K. R., Wong, N., Shinohara, M., & Miratrix, L. (2012). Differential effects of three professional development models on teacher knowledge and student achievement in elementary science. *Journal of Research in Science Teaching, 49*(3), 333–362.

Henry, G. T., Barrett, N., & Marder, C. (2016). "Double-dosing" in math in North Carolina public schools (REL 2016–140). Washington, DC: U.S. Department of Education, Institute of Education Sciences, National Center for Education Evaluation and Regional Assistance, Regional Educational Laboratory Southeast. Retrieved from http://ies.ed.gov/ncee/edlabs

Herman, J. L., & Linn, R. L. (2013). *On the road to assessing deeper learning: The status of Smarter Balanced and PARCC assessment consortia* (C RESST Report No. 823). Los Angeles: University of California, National Center for Research on Evaluation, Standards, and Student Testing.

Herman, J., & Linn, R. (2014). New assessments, new rigor. *Educational Leadership, 71*(6), 34–37.

Hoover, J. J. (2010). Special education eligibility decision making in response to intervention models. *Theory into Practice, 49*(4), 289–296.

Hughes, E. M. (2016). Core algebra instruction. In B. Witzel (Ed.), *Bridging the arithmetic to algebra gap for students with disabilities*. Arlington, VA: Council for Exceptional Children.

Hurst, S. (2014). *What is the difference between RTI and MTSS?* Retrieved from www.readinghorizons.com/blog/what-is-the-difference-between-rti-and-mtss

Individuals with Disabilities Education Improvement Act of 2004, Publ. No., 108–446, 118. Retrieved from http://idea.ed.gov/download/statute.html

Jenson, E. (2013). *Engaging students with poverty in mind: Practical strategies for raising achievement*. Alexandria, VA: Association for Supervision & Curriculum Development, Individuals with Disabilities Education Improvement Act of 2004, Publ. No., 08–446, 118.

Kirschner, P. A., Sweller, J., & Clark, R. E. (2006). Why minimal guidance during instruction does not work: An analysis of the failure of constructivist, discovery, problem-based, experiential, and inquiry-based teaching. *Educational Psychologist, 41*(2), 75–86.

Lalley, J. P., & Miller, R. H. (2006). Effects of pre-teaching and re-teaching on math achievement and academic self-concept of students with low achievement in math. *Education, 126*(4), 747–755.

Little, M. E. (2013). *RTI lesson planning & instructional decision-making: Keys to success in elementary classrooms.* New York: Dude Publishing.

Lochhead, J., & Whimbey, A. (1987). Teaching analytical reasoning through thinking aloud pair problem solving. In J. E. Stice (Ed.), *Developing critical thinking and problem-solving abilities, new directions for teaching and learning no. 30.* San Francisco: Jossey-Bass.

Loveless, T. (2014, February 19). What do we know about professional development? *Brookings.* Retrieved from www.brookings.edu/research/what-do-we-know-about-professional-development/

Marzano, R. J. (2004). *Building background knowledge for academic achievement: Research on what works in schools.* Alexandria, VA: ASCD.

Marzano, R. J., Pickering, D. J., & Pollock, J. E. (2001). *Classroom instruction that works.* Alexandria, VA: ASCD.

Marzano, R. J., & Toth, M. D. (2014). *Teaching for rigor: A call for a critical instructional shift.* West Palm Beach, FL: Learning Sciences International. Retrieved from www.marzanocenter.com/files/Teaching-for-Rigor-20140318.pdf

Menesses, K., & Gresham, F. (2009). Relative efficacy of reciprocal and nonreciprocal peer tutoring for students at-risk for academic failure. *School Psychology Quarterly, 24*(4). Retrieved from http://eds.a.ebscohost.com.winthropuniversity.idm.oclc.org/ehost

Moore, E. R., Sabousky, R., & Witzel, B. S. (2017). Meeting child find through response to intervention. *Childhood Education, 93*(4), 357–360.

National Association of Colleges and Employers. (2017). *Career readiness defined.* Retrieved from www.naceweb.org/career-readiness/competencies/career-readiness-defined/

National Commission on Excellence in Education (Ed.). (1983). *A nation at risk: The imperative for educational reform.* Washington, DC: Author.

National Reading Panel. (2000). *Teaching children to read: An evidence-based assessment of the scientific research literature on reading and its implications for reading instruction: Reports of the subgroups.* Washington, DC: National Institute of Child Health and Human Development.

Neitzel, J. (2010). Positive behavior supports for children and youth with autism spectrum disorders. *Preventing School Failure, 54*(4), 247–255.

Nese, R. N., Horner, R. H., Dickey, C. R., Stiller, B., & Tomlanovich, A. (2014). Decreasing bullying behaviors in middle school: Expect respect. *School Psychology Quarterly, 29*(3), 272–286.

Newman, L., Wagner, M., Knokey, A.-M., Marder, C., Nagle, K., Shaver, D., . . . Schwarting, M. (2011). The post-high school outcomes of young adults with disabilities up to 8 years after high school: A report from the National Longitudinal Transition Study-2 (NLTS2) (NCSER 2011–3005). Menlo Park, CA: SRI International.

North Carolina MTSS Leadership Team. (2016, September 9). Written interview with Dr. Brad Witzel.

Oregon Response to Intervention and Instruction. (2016, August 16). Written and personal interview with Dr. Brad Witzel.

Pew Research Center. (2017). Retrieved from www.pewresearch.org/fact-tank/2017/02/15/u-s-students-internationally-math-science/

Philibert, C. T. (2016). *Everyday SEL in elementary school.* New York: Routledge.

Pimentel, S. (April, 2013). *Promoting college and career-ready standards in adult basic education.* Washington, D.C.: MDR Associates, Inc. for the U.S. Department of Education.

Promoting College and Career-Ready Standards in Adult Basic Education. Retrieved from https://lincs.ed.gov/publications/pdf/CCRStandardsAdultEd.pdf

Reitman, D., Murphy, M., Hupp, S., & O'Callaghan, P. (2004). Behavior change and perceptions of change: Evaluating the effectiveness of a token economy. *Child & Family Behavior Therapy, 26*(2), 17–36.

Rodecki, J. N., & Witzel, B. S. (2011). Positively decreasing disruption and discipline referrals. *Focus on Middle School, 42*(2), 1–4.

Roderick, T. (2001). *A school of our own: Parents, power, and community at the east Harlem block schools.* New York: Teachers College Press.

Ronfeldt, M., Farmer, S. O., McQueen, K., & Grissom, J. A. (2015). Teacher collaboration in instructional teams and student achievement. *American Educational Research Journal, 52*(3), 475–514.

Ross, S. W., Horner, R. H., & Stiller, B. (2008). *Bully prevention in positive behavior support.* Eugene: Educational and Community Supports, University of Oregon. Retrieved from www.pbis.org/common/cms/files/pbisresources/pbsbullyprevention.pdf

Roth, K. J., Garnier, H. E., Chen, C., Lemmens, M., Schwille, K., & Wickler, N. I. Z. (2011). Videobased lesson analysis: Effective science PD for teacher and student learning. *Journal of Research in Science Teaching, 48*(2), 117–148.

Scammacca, N., Roberts, G., Vaughn, S., Edmonds, M., Wexler, J., Reutebuch, C. K., & Torgesen, J. K. (2007). *Interventions for adolescent struggling readers: A meta-analysis with implications for practice.* Portsmouth, NH: RMC Research Corporation, Center on Instruction.

Shanahan, T., Callison, K., Carriere, C., Duke, N. K., Pearson, P. D., Schatschneider, C., & Torgesen, J. (2010). *Improving reading comprehension in kindergarten through 3rd grade: A practice guide* (NCEE 2010–4038). Washington, DC: National Center for Education Evaluation and Regional Assistance, Institute of Education Sciences, U.S. Department of Education.

Sherrod, M., Getch, Y., & Ziomek-Daigle, J. (2009). The impact of positive behavior support to decrease discipline referrals with elementary students. *Professional School Counseling, 12*(6), 421–427.

Stecker, P. M., Fuchs, D., & Fuchs, L. S. (2008). Progress monitoring as essential practice within response to intervention. *Rural Special Education Quarterly, 27*(4), 10–17.

Stecker, P. M., Lembke, E. S., & Foegen, A. (2008). Using progress-monitoring data to improve instructional decision making. *Preventing School Failure, 52*(2), 48–58.

Tantillo, C. (2016). *Everyday SEL.* New York: Routledge.

Turnbull, B. (2002). Teacher participation and buy-in: Implications for school reform initiatives. *Learning Environments Research, 5*(3), 235–252.

U.S. Department of Education, National Center for Education Statistics. (2016). *Digest of education statistics, 2015* (NCES 2016–014), Chapter 2. Retrieved from https://nces.ed.gov/fastfacts/display.asp?id=64

Wallace Foundation. (2011). *The school principal as leader: Guiding schools to better teaching and learning.* Retrieved from www.wallacefoundation.org/knowledge-center/school-leadership/effective-principal-leadership/Documents/The-School-Principal-as-Leader-Guiding-Schools-to-Better-Teaching-and-Learning.pdf

Whitten, E., Esteves, K. J., & Woodrow, A. (2009). *RTI success.* Minneapolis, MN: Free Spirit.

Wiedemann, T. (2016, August 28). Written interview with Dr. Brad Witzel.

Williamson, G. L. (2006). Aligning the journey with a destination: A model for K–16 reading standards (Lexile Framework for Reading White paper). Durham, NC: MetaMetrics.

Williamson, A., & Witzel, B. S. (2016) Instilling resilience in children of poverty. *The Winthrop McNair Research Bulletin, 2(13).* Available at http://digitalcommons.winthrop.edu/wmrb/vol2/iss1/13/?utm_source=digitalcommons.winthrop.edu%2Fwmrb%2Fvol2%2Fiss1%2F13&utm_medium=PDF&utm_campaign=PDFCoverPages.

Williamson, R., & Blackburn, B. R. (2010). *Rigorous Schools and Classrooms: Leading the Way.* New York: Routledge.

Williamson, R., & Blackburn, B. R. (2011). *Rigor in your school: A toolkit for leaders* (1st ed). New York: Routledge.

Williamson, R., & Blackburn, B. (2017). *Rigor in your school: A toolkit for leaders* (2nd ed.). New York: Routledge.

Witzel, B. S. (2007). Using contingent praise to engage students in inclusive classrooms. *Teachers as Leaders, 7,* 27–32.

Witzel, B. S., & Little, M. E. (2016). *Teaching elementary mathematics to struggling learners.* New York: Guilford.

Woodward, J., Beckmann, S., Driscoll, M., Franke, M., Herzig, P., Jitendra, A., Koedinger, K. R., & Ogbuehi, P. (2012). *Improving mathematical problem solving in grades 4 through 8: A practice guide* (NCEE 2012–4055). Washington, DC: National Center for Education Evaluation and Regional Assistance, Institute of Education Sciences, U.S. Department of Education.